FIRST LADY

FIRST LADY

A PLAY IN THREE ACTS

by

KATHARINE DAYTON

and

GEORGE S. KAUFMAN

ACTING EDITION

RANDOM HOUSE · NEW YORK

NOTE

"FIRST LADY"

MANUFACTURED IN THE UNITED STATES OF AMERICA

"First Lady" was produced by Sam H. Harris at the Music Box Theatre, New York, on Tuesday night, November 26th, 1935, with the following cast:

Sophy Prescott	DIANTHA PATTISON
Charles	JAMES SEELEY
Emmy Paige	HELEN BROOKS
Lucy Chase Wayne	JANE COWL
Stephen Wayne	STANLEY RIDGES
Belle Hardwick	JESSIE BUSLEY
Mrs. Ives	REGINA WALLACE
Ann Forrester	RITA VALE
A Congressman's Wife	MARGHERITA SARGENT
Her Friend	LESLIE BINGHAM
The Baroness	ULLA KAZANOVA
Señor Ortega	ARMAND CORTES
A Chinese	HON. WU
A General	DONALD MCKENZIE
Mrs. Creevey	ETHEL WILSON
Mrs. Davenport	LILLIAN NORTON
Senator Keane	JUDSON LAIRE
Tom Hardwick	THOMAS FINDLAY
Irene Hibbard	LILY CAHILL
Bleecker	JOHN M. TROUGHTON
Carter Hibbard	OSWALD YORKE
George Mason	FRANK DAE
Ellsworth T. Ganning	FLORENZ AMES
Jason Fleming	DON BEDDOE
Herbert Sedgwick	GEORGE PARSONS

Guests at the Reception, Butlers, etc.—ISIS BRINN, SUSAN POWERS, CHARLES LaRUE, DANIEL OCKO, NAOE KONDO and BRADFORD HUNT.

Stage Manager—WILLIAM MacFADDEN

THE SCENES

ACT ONE

Living room in the Secretary of State's Home. Washington, D. C., December.

ACT TWO

Scene I. Carter Hibbard's Study. January.

Scene II. The Secretary of State's Home. February.

ACT THREE

Again the Secretary's Home. March.

FIRST LADY

ACT I

*Living room in the Secretary of State's home,
Washington, D. C. It is a cluttered, homelike room
—not "done" in any particular period, but a mix-
ture of three generations. Charming, old-fashioned.
Solid American.*

*Dominating the room is the portrait of a vigorous,
middle-aged man, painted somewhere around the
turn of the century. Somehow you sense that from
this old fellow have stemmed the family traditions and position.*

*Across a hall at the rear you get a glimpse of the
dining-room, set for tea with silver service,
candles, flowers, etc. As the curtain rises the second* BUTLER *enters* U.L. *in dining-room, and places
a pile of plates on the table. Exits* U.L. CHARLES,
first butler, enters U.L.

After a moment there enters D.L. *an attractive,
poised woman, somewhere in her thirties. Her
name is* SOPHY PRESCOTT. *She brings a little stack
of ash receivers and scatters them around the
room, first on table* R., *then on what-not* U.C. *of
arch, and finally on desk* L., *replacing others obviously more valuable. That done, she calls to the
senior* BUTLER. *After* SOPHY *puts down first ashtray, she turns light switch.*

(LIGHTS ON BRACKETS.)

SOPHY. Charles!

CHARLES. (*Crossing down to her.*) Yes, Miss Prescott?

7

SOPHY. (*Handing him the 3 ash receivers.*) Put these ash-trays away, will you?

CHARLES. Yes'm.

SOPHY. If they must have souvenirs let them steal these. I'm not going to have them carrying off bits of jade and ivory, the way they usually do.

CHARLES. I always try to watch, Miss, but there are so many ladies.

SOPHY. I know, Charles. (*She peers into a cigarette box on table* D.R.) Where are those cigarettes the Persian Minister sent? We must have those out where he can see them.

CHARLES. On the table, Miss. And I put Egyptians in the other compartment in case the Egyptian Minister comes. (*He starts to go. Her voice stops him.*)

SOPHY. That was very diplomatic, Charles. Well, we're all ready. Flowers, Egyptians, Persians, teatable, candles, souvenir ashtrays—all we need is a hostess. Charles, was that all that Mrs. Wayne said? Just that she was at the Senate?

CHARLES. Yes, Miss. Listening to Senator Keane's speech.

(*There enters* U.L. *a soft and fluffy young woman—very young, naïve, Southern.* EMMY PAIGE.)

SOPHY. (*Furiously, as she takes up the telephone.*) Senator Keane's speech! (*Into phone.*) National 3120.

EMMY. (*Very, very Southern.*) Isn't Aunt Lucy home yet?

SOPHY. Oh, Charles! Edward should be on the door soon. Or maybe you'd better let Edward help you and put one of the caterer's men on the door—that oldish one with the mole on his chin. (CHARLES *exits* U.L.) (*To* EMMY.) You know, he looked so unappetizing at the Herricks' dinner last night, but it won't matter at the door. Hello!

EMMY. Oh, I know the one you mean. You know, it took me the longest time to figure out why everybody in Washington had a butler with a mole on his chin. Then I found out it was the same one.

SOPHY. (*Sits at desk.*) Hello! Capitol? . . . Senate Press, please.

EMMY. (*Purling on.*) I declare, some of them are such distinguished-looking men, and you meet 'em at everybody's parties. I don't know half the time whether they're butlers or some old Senator. I don't see how you ever tell!

SOPHY. (*Through her teeth.*) The butlers don't talk, Emmy. . . . Hello! Mr. Halloran? . . . This is Sophy Prescott. . . . Thank you, just fine. . . . Mr. Halloran, would you look over at the Senators' gallery and see if Mrs. Wayne has left? I think she's listening to Senator Keane's speech!

EMMY. I don't see how Aunt Lucy can sit in that old Senate all the time. I'd think she'd just scr-ream! I was talking to Paul Starrett about her and he says she knows what those old Senators are saying when they don't even know themselves. He says—

SOPHY. (EMMY *drifts* R.) Hello! . . . Oh, she's still there? Well, how long has Senator Keane been speaking? . . . I see . . . Well, if he *does* stop will you tell Mrs. Wayne to come right home? . . . That she's wanted here . . . No, nothing serious. Just tell her to come home. Thank you, so much! (*She hangs up—her fury breaks out. Rises.*) No, nothing serious! Nothing but the official day at home of the wife of the Secretary of State, that's all! Nothing but that any minute everybody in Washington will be pouring in here, from ex-Presidents' widows to Armenian atrocities! And those damnable delegates! Oh, how I hate delegates! (*Pacing back and forth.*)

EMMY. What delegates?

SOPHY. The Women's Peace, Purity and Patriotism League, God bless their homes! I wish they'd stay in 'em!

EMMY. (*Sits L. of table.*) Oh, I know the ones you mean. They were having lunch at the Mayflower today—they all had on big blue and gold sashes!

SOPHY. (*Sits at desk.*) Those are the ones!

EMMY. Paul Starrett says to look at how big they are, patriotism must be an awful healthy profession!

SOPHY. Look here—where have you been seeing Paul Starrett so much?

EMMY. We just had lunch today. Sometimes we have lunch, and he tells me funny stories about people.

SOPHY. (*Turns to* EMMY.) And you tell *him,* I suppose?

EMMY. (*Innocently.*) Huh?

SOPHY. You tell him funny stories about your Aunt Lucy?

EMMY. (*Rises and crosses to* C.) Why, Sophy, I do not.

SOPHY. I knew it. I knew it the minute I picked up that column of his this morning. With Lucy's remark about Irene Hibbard being the Ten Least-Dressed Women in Washington.

EMMY. Well, Aunt Lucy did say it, and everybody laughed. She says terrible wrong things, and people always laugh. (*Crossing to* R.)

SOPHY. But she says them at the right time, Emmy, and to the right people.

EMMY. Well, down in Mississippi everybody tells everybody everything, and nothing happens except once in a while somebody shoots somebody.

SOPHY. Well, if that's all that happened here . . .

(WARN PHONE. WARN DOOR SLAM.)

EMMY. I declare I think Washington's awful confusin'. All that about where you sit, and who sits next to who—I don't see how you ever learned it. Aunt Lucy says you're the best secretary in Washington. She says if it wasn't for you she doesn't know what she'd do.

SOPHY. The same as she does now, probably—whatever she feels like.

EMMY. (*Sits* L. *of table.*) That's what Paul Starrett said. He thinks Aunt Lucy is the most glamorous woman—he says he doesn't see how she has a niece like me. I mean, he thinks she's so young-looking.

SOPHY. Oh! I see.

EMMY. So I said, I'm just her niece by marriage, and he said, Oh, *that* was how it happened!

SOPHY. Well, Emmy, please don't tell him anything more. Especially not about your Aunt and Irene Hibbard!

EMMY. He says Aunt Lucy and Mrs. Hibbard are the two most glamorous women in Washington and no wonder they're enemies! (*She sighs deeply.*) I wish I knew how you *got* glamorous! I remember when I first heard Uncle Stephen was engaged to Lucy Chase. I like to died it was so glamorous. President Chase being her grandfather— (*Her eyes involuntarily go to the portrait*)—and living in the White House and all.

(*The telephone rings.*) (EMMY *occupies herself curling her hair with the paper-knife.*)   (PHONE.)

SOPHY. (*Pouncing.*) Hello! (*Obviously disappointed.*) Yes, this is Miss Prescott. . . . No, just the same list the evening

papers have. . . . Why, it was certainly sent to you at the
Herald, Miss Jones. . . . Well, you might mention the
Women's Peace, Purity and Patriotism League—The Secretary of State and Mrs. Wayne are particularly happy to
have them as guests today . . . Why she's wearing—(*She
looks at her watch—makes a quick decision*)—she's wearing
Pompeiian crepe!

EMMY. (*Rises and crosses to* SOPHY. *In a quick whisper.*)
Oh, no!

SOPHY. (*Silencing her with a wave of the hand.*) That's right
—the same one she wore at the Pan-American reception.
With the emerald pendant. . . . Yes, it is nice. . . . It was
a gift to her from the Latin-American Republics when her
grandfather was in the White House. . . . Not at all, Miss
Jones. (*She hangs up.*)

EMMY. But she won't wear that gown, Sophy.

SOPHY. You bet she'll wear it! She'll wear rubber boots
and rompers if I tell the newspaper women she's going to.
(*Slams down paper-weight. Rises.*) Really, I could kill her!
She's spoiled that's what's the matter with her! Lucy Chase,
the White House baby! She's the most maddening, self-
willed, unreliable—   (DOOR SLAM.)

(*There is the slam of a door downstairs. The eyes of both
SOPHY and EMMY go to the entrance hall. CHARLES appears
in the dining-room doorway. For a moment they all stand
waiting. LUCY CHASE WAYNE comes in. Having spent her
girlhood in the White House, a hundred and twenty million
people know her age, but you would never think it to look
at her. She has good looks, but they are subordinate to her
vitality, charm, distinction. She carries an extra large handbag. Over the years every newspaper and magazine in
America has printed her picture—not once, but again and
again. Everything she does, everything she says, is News.*)

Should her dog bite the most obscure man in the world, it gets a box on Page One. She is Lucy Chase Wayne.)

LUCY. (*Looks over dining-room* U.C. *Puts bag on table* D.R.) Oh, how lovely everything looks! How nice, Charles! The table looks beautiful!   You've arranged everything divinely! Emmy, child, you look charming!   Thanks, Charles.   Oh, so many flowers. Looks like a gunman's funeral. (*Looking toward drawing-room* D.L. *As she gets rid of her coat* SOPHY *starts to speak.* CHARLES *exits* U.L.) Now, Sophy darling, don't say it! You'll only be sorry, and besides I can take the words right out of your mouth. Such an unsanitary phrase, isn't it? "It was all very well when you were Lucy Chase, or even Lucy Chase Wayne," etc., etc.,—curtain lowered to denote the passing of two hours—"but now that you are the wife of a Cabinet member"—Sophy, don't look so grim— can't you ever forget you were General Prescott's daughter? (*Takes a cigarette from box on table.*) You shouldn't scold me—I've been saving the country. . . . Wouldn't you think Marconi or somebody would invent a bag you could find matches in?

SOPHY. Lucy, *will* you go up and dress?

LUCY. All right, but give me a breathing spell. (EMMY *lights cigarette for* LUCY.) Thank you, dear. Sitting up in that Senate for two hours. I've got his speech somewhere. (*She is still delving into the bag.*) Sophy, you must get me another copy of the Constitution—this is *so* ratty-looking. (EMMY *sits* R. *of table.*)

SOPHY. Lucy, please!

LUCY. Do you know what he was going to do, Sophy? Keane, I mean. He was going to make a speech attacking Stephen's treaties. If I hadn't headed him off. . . . Where's Stephen? Isn't he home yet?

SOPHY. (*Crossing to the desk.*) He phoned a little while ago. And there are some flowers on your dressing-table.

LUCY. My darling old elephant—he never forgets.

EMMY. I saw Senator Keane once. He's right good-looking.

LUCY. Emmy, ask Charles to bring me some tea up in my room—right now, while I'm dressing. It'll be hours before I get any.

EMMY. (*On her way, crossing up above table to arch.*) All right. Gordon Keane—that's his name. He's the Boy Senator from that old State out West.

LUCY. Must you talk in captions, Emmy?

EMMY. Well, of course, I expect he wouldn't be a boy any-where but in the Senate. I mean not at Annapolis or in the movies or anything. Because he's awful good-looking to be in the Senate. (*Exits* U.L.)

LUCY. (*Cross to* C.) Boy Senator! That's really just what he is, Sophy. I think that whole Western crowd is just using him, and Irene's helping them to do it. But he's not going to upset those treaties. They're the dearest things to Stephen's heart, and I'm not going to let anybody monkey with them.

SOPHY. (*Crosses to* C., *pencil, letters, lists in her hands.*) Now, Lucy, hadn't you better go easy with Keane? Irene Hibbard is entirely too close to him.

LUCY. Well, she isn't as close as she was, Sophy.

SOPHY. Oh, dear! Now what?

LUCY. Well, it seems Irene lunches with him pretty nearly every day, only today I got there first. If you could have seen her face when she came into the Senate restaurant. Her nostrils positively breathed fire—you could have cooked

crepes suzette over them. Just then old Senator Taylor
came in and she wound up having lunch with *him—you*
know, he's a hundred and seven. They made an ideal couple.
He had milk toast.

SOPHY. Lucy, when are you going to grow up?

LUCY. But the main thing is: I got him to change the
speech—Keane. He didn't *even mention* Stephen's treaties.
I watched Irene while he was talking and she was furious.
If you ask me she put him up to the whole thing. She was
taking a jab at *me,* through Stephen.

SOPHY. You don't really believe that.

LUCY. Why not? How about that last little trick of hers—
wrecking my dinner party by kidnapping that foul
little royal jackass—my guest of honor three hours late,
all because her car broke down! Her car! If you ask me
that wasn't all that broke down. (*Crosses to* D.R.)

SOPHY. All right, all right, Lucy. But *won't* you go up now?

LUCY. You know, there's something behind this Keane business, Sophy. She's pushing him right into *her* crowd—every
chance she gets. And this speech today. There's something
behind it. By the way, look out for him this afternoon, if
I'm tied up when he gets here.

SOPHY. When who gets here?

LUCY. Keane, of course.

SOPHY. He's coming here?

LUCY. Of course he is—what do you think I've been doing?
I want Stephen to talk to him—we've got to get him into
our camp.

SOPHY. Does Irene know he's coming here?

LUCY. I hope so. I devoutly hope so. . . . Well! (*A move as though to go; stops again as she sees the little pile of cards on the table,* D.R.) What's all this?

SOPHY. Just flowers.

LUCY. (*Running through the cards.*) Senator and Mrs. Daggett, roses; Senator and Mrs. Waldron, roses; the Minister of Portugal and Madame De Silva, roses; Señor Don Claudio Lozano—oh, yes, Bolivia—roses; Representative and Mrs. Button, *roses*. (STEPHEN WAYNE *has appeared in the doorway, carrying a brief-case. Of thoroughly dignified yet pleasing appearance. That bit of grey at the temples.*) Stephen, darling. (*She kisses him.*) And another for your flowers. (*She kisses him again.* SOPHY *exits* D.L.) I haven't seen them yet, but I know they're not roses.

STEPHEN. (*Dropping brief-case in chair* L. *of table.*) Well? All ready for the great invasion?

LUCY. Stephen dear, you look tired. That miserable State Department is wearing you out. What was it—those French and English again?

STEPHEN. Oh, it's not as bad as all that.

LUCY. But it is. They began phoning you at six o'clock this morning—I heard it. And it was the same yesterday.

STEPHEN. Well, that can't be helped. Don't forget when it's six o'clock in Washington, it's already eleven in London. You can't blame the British for the change in time, my dear.

LUCY. Well, let them stay up *later* or something. Why does it always have to be *you?*

STEPHEN. It's only for a little while. This is a special occasion.

LUCY. It's always a special occasion. You've worn your working clothes every day this week. Look! (*A gesture to-*

ward his cutaway and striped trousers.) You know what we're going to do?

STEPHEN. No—what?

LUCY. The minute those treaties are signed we're going away some place—just you and I—some place where there aren't any foreigners or any Americans.

STEPHEN. What'll you do about cables?

LUCY. Cables? What do they say, anyhow? "Love and kisses —Mussolini." "Cheerio—Anthony Eden." We'll go where they can't find you.

STEPHEN. (*With a little laugh.*) I'm afraid there's no such place. And what would you do about all your Senators and things? You know you can't live without them.

LUCY. Darling, I don't really care about anything in the world but you, and you know it. (*She kisses him.*)

STEPHEN. (*Kisses her hand.*) Bless you.

LUCY. And that reminds me—I think I've got a new Senator for you. (*Crosses L. to desk.*) You've got to be very nice to him. Tell him you heard he made a very good speech this afternoon.

STEPHEN. Did he?

LUCY. Wonderful—I practically wrote it.

STEPHEN. (*Standing L. of table D.R.*) Now, darling, I wish you'd give up ghost writing for Senators. You know it always gets you into trouble.

LUCY. But you can't let Senators write their *own* speeches, Stephen.

STEPHEN. (*A step toward LUCY.*) Well, give them a chance once in a while. Remember what happened with the soldiers' bonus, when you almost disrupted the Navy by getting old Senator Whozis to come out for a *sailors'* bonus?

LUCY. Well, I still think it was a good idea. They work much harder than the soldiers—polishing that brass all the time. And I was going to get the brass polish people to pay for the bonus.

STEPHEN. (*Back of table.*) Oh, I'm sure you had it all worked out.

LUCY. Well, it really wasn't bad. The Navy liked it—remember Norfolk? They were going to give me a salute of twenty-two guns.

STEPHEN. Yes, that would have been fine. That's just one more than they give the President.

LUCY. Oh, he never would have known it. He always has his fingers in his ears.

STEPHEN. No, Lucy, the more I think about it the more I think you'd better give up your official writing career. You're really much safer with a sword than with a pen. (*Bus. of opening brief-case.*)

LUCY. Well, if you want the country to go to the dogs. . . .

STEPHEN. You know, it's really a good thing you weren't around when the Constitution was written. Lord knows what you'd have done to *that.*

LUCY. Well, if I had been it wouldn't need so much work *now.* (STEPHEN *yawns.*) . . . Darling, why don't you lie down a few minutes, with this mob coming? You look *so* tired. I'll bet you didn't have a bite of lunch, did you?

STEPHEN (*Crossing to* LUCY.) Yes, I did.

LUCY. What? One of those brought-in sandwiches?

STEPHEN. Not at all. As a matter of fact, I had lunch with the President.

LUCY. Really? What did he say?

STEPHEN. Nothing.

LUCY. Now, Stephen. He couldn't have a whole lunch and say nothing.

STEPHEN. Well, he—said it was a nice day. Asked after *you*—

LUCY. Stephen, you're *so* aggravating. You only tell me the things you want me to know.

STEPHEN. (*Drifts back to table.*) Well, that's all we tell Great Britain.   (WARNING LIGHTS *and* DOOR BELL.)

LUCY. Really, it's terrible being married to the Secretary of State. His whole business is not telling things.

STEPHEN. You know I'd tell you anything I could, Lucy. You also know I *want* to tell you *every*thing.

LUCY (*Suddenly serious.*) Then why don't you?

STEPHEN. (*Taken aback.*) Well— (*Crossing to* LUCY.)

LUCY. Oh, I don't mean state secrets, Stephen. What did the President say about you? (*Slight turn of head from* STEPHEN.) Because I know, Stephen—I feel it. It was about *you,* wasn't it? He wants you to succeed *him.* We've never talked about it, Stephen—all these years. It's been— too deep down to talk about. Whenever anybody's mentioned it—your being President, I mean—we've just laughed. We've never really talked about it.

STEPHEN. (*With quiet dignity.*) And we never *must* talk about it, Lucy.

LUCY. But I want to talk about it, Stephen. I want you to have it. So much. You've worked so hard, Stephen. You've been so good. Oh, dear, you *are* so good.

STEPHEN. Do you really want it as badly as all that, my dear?

LUCY. (*They break.*) Oh, not for myself, Stephen. It'd be no treat for me—I know what mother went through. But I want it for you, Stephen—for you and the country. They need you, Stephen.

STEPHEN. Oh, I think they'll stagger along, Lucy—even without me. But I appreciate your giving me the nomination. I'd rather be your choice than the people's, any day.

(STEPHEN *looks at her for a moment, the ghost of a smile on his lips. Then he leans forward and kisses her, ever so gently, as* SOPHY *reenters,* D.L., *bringing two open boxes containing corsages.*)

SOPHY. Do you want to take a look at these?

(STEPHEN *crosses to table, picks up his brief-case and starts* U.C.)

LUCY. What? . . . Oh, for me? His Excellency! (*To* STEPHEN.) Paying the war debts in orchids.

STEPHEN. Well, all I can say is he's got to send a hell of a lot of them. (*He exits* U.L.)

LUCY. (*Bringing out an enormous spray of gardenias, tied with a red-white-and-blue ribbon with gold letters.*) Oh, my God, Sophy! What's this? (*Taking spray out of box.*)

SOPHY. It's from the W.P.P.P., and you've got to wear it.

LUCY. (*Scanning card.*) Peace, Purity and Patriotism. *They're* coming!

SOPHY. In hordes.

LUCY. My dear, they're priceless! The Capitol just teemed with them this morning—they were riding herd on all the Senators. Their president was a large, dovey lady, an absolute symbol of peace—I suppose this is she— (*She reads the card.*) "Mrs. Louella May Creevey." . . . Creevey, Sophy . . .   (DOOR BELL.)

(*A* BUTLER *passes along the hallway* U.L. *to* U.R. *and switches on hall chandelier.*)   (LIGHTS CHANDELIER.)
       (START TO DIM OFF STAGE LIGHTING RIGHT.)

SOPHY. (*Crossing* U.C.) Now, you see! And nobody on the door yet! Lucy, *will* you go?   (*Close to door* U.R.C.)

LUCY. Yes, darling. But it's only Belle Hardwick or some other tea pourer. I won't be five minutes. (*Getting her handbag on table* D.R.)

SOPHY. And by the way, you're wearing your Pompeiian.

       (WARN CANDLES)

LUCY. Who said so?

SOPHY. I said so. To the newspaper women. And I'm not going to have those girls on my neck again.

LUCY. It's too absurd. Can't I even wear what I want?

SOPHY. Not when I've already told the newspapers.

LUCY. (*Resigned.*) Oh, very well! If I've gone to press I've gone to press. (*She picks up the* CREEVEY *flowers.*) But surely I don't have to wear *this?*

SOPHY. You certainly do. Those women would never forgive you!

LUCY. All right, General Prescott! If you want me to look like Arlington on Decoration Day! (*She presses the flowers to her bosom as she departs* U.L.)

(CHARLES *comes in* D.L., *bearing a great stack of flower boxes.*)

SOPHY. No, Charles! No! Take them away. (*Putting two corsage boxes on top of* CHARLES' *stack of boxes. He takes them out again.*)

(SECOND BUTLER *enters* U.R. *and lights the six candles on dining-room table. Exits* U.L.)   (LIGHT CANDLES.)

(*The first reception* GUESTS *arrive. They are, as* LUCY *has predicted, a couple of assisting tea pourers—by name,* MRS. BELLE HARDWICK *and* MRS. IVES. *The former is an ample woman somewhere in her fifties;* MRS. IVES *is a few years younger.*)

BELLE. (*Enters* U.R.) Hello, Sophy darling! I see we're the first ones!

MRS. IVES. (*Sits* L. *of table.*) Where's your tea party? Hello, Sophy!

SOPHY. Oh, I'm so glad it's *you!* How are you, Belle? Hello, Mary!

BELLE. Where's Lucy? Not here yet?

SOPHY. She'll be down in a minute. Thank heavens for you nice dependable women.

MRS. IVES. (*Crossing* U.R. *of table.*) You know, I'd like just once to get to one of Lucy's parties after *she* does.

(SOPHY *over to desk.*)

BELLE. Well, I'm *always* early. Just an old Washington war-horse minding her protocol and precedence. I wasn't a White House child; *I* haven't got any of that fiendish Chase charm, so I *have* to be early. I have to call and be called upon. Do you know how many calling cards I used last year? Five *thousand!* (*She picks up a cigarette with brilliant red tip—the Egyptian contribution.*) Don't you love red tips? If Tom gets the Senate again this Fall I'm going to relax for six years and order some of those. (*Puts cigarette back in box.*)

MRS. IVES. (*Sits* R. *of table. Reading the printed words on one of the cigarettes.*) "Le Khédive. Alexandria, Egypt."

(SOPHY *sits arm of desk chair.*)

BELLE. *You* could use them, Mary— Cabinet members don't run for office. But *our* State! My dear, they have kidnappers and rape and more general hell-raising than you can shake a stick at, but their politicians' home lives must be pure. Caesar's wife was a hussy compared to what a Senator's wife from our State has to be. If I smoked these at home, Tom would lose the election sure. Oh, well! I haven't done anything I wanted to for thirty-five years. I've been running for office, first with father and then with Tom Hardwick, till my tongue's hanging out.

SOPHY. You love it, Belle—you know you do. And you love all this Washington thing—that's why you do it so beautifully, and why you'll be coming back here, Allah be praised, long after people have stopped voting for Tom.

BELLE. Oh, no. I'll never come back here an "ex"-anything. (*Rises, crosses* L.) If I get carried out of Washington in a ballot box I'm going to *stay* out. . . . What do you want me to do this afternoon, Sophy?

SOPHY. (*Sitting on arm of desk chair.*) Oh, just push everybody into the dining-room and then push them right out again.

BELLE. I suppose everybody'll be here—especially the foreigners. They always turn out for Lucy the way they do for a royal funeral.

MRS. IVES. Yes, the State Department has all the luck. All I get on my days are post-office officials and Congressmen's wives!

BELLE. Me, too!

(ANN FORRESTER *enters. Young, attractive; a State Department wife.*)

ANN. Oh, good, I'm not late! (*She greets the older women; makes the rounds gracefully.*)

BELLE. (*Sits back of table.*) Oh, hello, darling, how are you?

MRS. IVES. Hello, there!

ANN. Good afternoon, Mrs. Hardwick, Mary— Miss Prescott!

(*Simultaneously.*)

SOPHY. (*In the hallway.*) Hello, Ann. Lucy, aren't you nearly ready? (*She exits* U.L.)

ANN. What a time! I've been packing Wallace to go down the bay and meet the President of Haiti, and you can't imagine what it means. His boat reaches Quarantine at an ungodly hour—that means a sack suit to meet the boat in, and changing to cutaway on the train for the reception at the station. If I've forgotten anything it practically means war, because the smaller and blacker the country the fussier they are.

MRS. IVES. You shouldn't be nervous after the way you handled the Abyssinians last summer. They don't come any blacker than that.

ANN. That nightmare! Oh, dear! Ninety-eight in the shade, Wallace in his morning coat, and the Abyssinian Prince in simple leopard skins and diamonds. . . . You know, I just love this room. There are just three rooms in Washington that have real American atmosphere—the little old Supreme Court chamber—I don't know why they ever left it—and the Blue Room at the White House, and this. And I think I like this best of all.

MRS. IVES. It's that portrait of old President Chase. Somehow he's still presiding.

ANN. Well, that's part of it, of course! (*Her eyes linger on it for a moment.*) You know, Mrs. Wayne has that same look around the eyes, hasn't she? Or rather behind the eyes. But, of course, she gets her beauty from her mother. Oh, that heavenly portrait in the drawing-room.

BELLE. She was an angel if ever there was one.

MRS. IVES. I wish I'd been here then. She must have been a very clever woman.

BELLE. (*To* IVES.) Mm. She handed the old (*To* ANN.) President like nobody's business. And she had something else besides cleverness. Kindness. It's a combination that's rare in Washington—cleverness and kindness. But it makes wonderful hostesses!

ANN. (*Sitting on arm of chair* L. *of table.*) What makes us so unkind, anyhow? I suppose nobody lasts here long enough to feel that it really matters. The whole place shifting with every administration. . . . You know the people you meet aren't going to be here a couple of years from now, and you aren't either. So why should you bother?

MRS. IVES. But it's a lot of fun while you are in town here. Of course, it's a lot like home in some ways—every bit as hick, really, and always a feud going on, with everybody in town lining up on one side or the other. You've got to be for either the first or the second wife in every divorce, just like at home. But the difference is that everybody's *somebody* here—it puts gossip on a much higher plane, somehow. There's a finish to it, if you know what I mean.

BELLE. And yet the dirt's all there, underneath!

MRS. IVES. (*Rises.*) Exactly! Take Lucy and Irene, for instance. Back home they'd just be any two Methodists, but here it's Lucy Chase Wayne and Mrs. Hibbard, the wife of a Supreme Court Justice. My dear, I trembled at the Roumanian Legation the other night. They just missed each other by two minutes!

ANN. You should have seen them up at the Capitol today—nobody listened to poor Senator Keane. Every eye in the place was on the gallery!

MRS. IVES. What do you mean? They weren't together, surely?

ANN. Heavens, no!

MRS. IVES. I guess it's one feud we can count on, year after year. What started it, anyhow? A man?

BELLE. Naturally.

MRS. IVES. Really?

ANN. Secretary Wayne?

BELLE. No, indeed. Taking a woman's husband—that's fair enough—everybody expects that—but Irene did worse. (*To* MRS. IVES.) She took Lucy's cook.

MRS. IVES. Why, I never heard that.

BELLE. (*To* IVES.) Well, that's how it started. He was a colored chef. He made the most heavenly omelets . . . popovers . . . batter-bread and roe-herring . . . you'd wake up in the night dreaming about them. They made Lucy's Sunday breakfasts the most potent political force in Washington—(*To* ANN.) Presidents were made and unmade, right between popovers. . . . And then Irene came along. She'd just divorced that foreign prince of hers—what was his name?

MRS. IVES. Gregoravitch.

BELLE. That's it. I never can remember.

MRS. IVES. I don't see how you can forget. He's always marrying somebody.

BELLE. Anyhow, she took that house on Massachusetts Avenue, and started in to splurge with the Baker millions—she was born Irene Baker in Mansfield, Ohio—her father made those old Baker Steamers—you know, the wrong kind of automobile, while Henry Ford was making the right kind —but they made an awful lot of money before too many of them blew up.

MRS. IVES. Oh, I'll never catch up on Washington. But of course I've only been here two administrations.

BELLE. (*Rising.*) Well, man and boy I've seen eight, which makes me practically a Neanderthal woman. When you've seen only two you think they're different, (*starts* L.) but by the time you see eight you know they're all alike.

ANN. But so much happens.

BELLE. Yes, a lot happens, but nothing changes. No matter how big the personality it always passes. It's Washington itself that stays.

(LUCY, *finally dressed for the occasion, appears in the hallway. Charming, dignified, beautifully gowned, big bag of material blending with gown, flowers attractively pinned on.* SOPHY *is behind her* U.L. *with* W.P.P.P. *corsage.*)

(WARN CLOCK STRIKE.)

MRS. IVES. Mrs. Wayne.

ANN. Good afternoon. (*She rises.*)

LUCY. I'm so sorry, but Sophy never told me you were here! Sophy, why do you do those things? Belle, what a lovely hat!

BELLE. Now, Lucy, relax.

LUCY. No, really—

SOPHY. (*Closing doors part way.*) Oh, good Lord, here they come. *Mobs* of them.

LUCY. Well, close the doors—quick. (SOPHY *closes them and exits* D.L.) Ann, Stephen tells me that Wallace is doing the most marvelous work on the Trans-Bulgaria treaty.

ANN. I'm so glad!

LUCY. Mary, darling, tell the Postmaster General he ought to put you on a stamp, just the way you look!

MRS. IVES. Now, Mrs. Wayne.

LUCY. They're going to send us all their caviar and all we're going to give them is a lot of old shoes or something.

SOPHY. (*Entering* D.L.) Are you ready, Lucy? The room is filling up.

LUCY. Come on, girls—up and at 'em! Belle, I want you in there. Mary, you'd better start in the hall. You, too, Ann. And remember, keep people moving. That's the secret of the whole thing. It doesn't matter where they go, so long as they keep moving. (MRS. IVES *starts off,* ANN *follows, and as they open the center doors a little and squeeze through there is a glimpse of arriving guests in the hallway; the buzz of conversation. Exit* U.C.) Oooh! Sounds like a bird store! Sophy, keep those doors closed—we'll use this room as a haven. Sophy, don't let that Peace and Purity woman get past me. (SOPHY *exits* D.L. *as* LUCY *starts off with* BELLE.) Once I accidentally snubbed a temperance woman and it delayed repeal three years.

(SHE *and* BELLE *exit* D.L.)

(MRS. IVES *comes busily in from the hall* U.R. *Immediately as the doors open a great buzz springs up in the dining room.*

You get a glimpse of WOMEN *milling.* MRS. IVES *exits to drawing room* D.L. *As* MRS. IVES *reaches stage Center, clock strikes five.*)

(*Then* LUCY *comes into view again,* D.L., *piloting a couple of* WOMEN.)

LUCY. Why yes, of course you may! That's Grandfather's picture right over there.

THE FIRST WOMAN. Oh, thank you, Mrs. Wayne! Thank you ever so much!

THE SECOND WOMAN. (*As* LUCY *disappears again* D.L.) Thank you. . . . Isn't she lovely? I don't believe half those stories about her, do you?

THE FIRST WOMAN. We'd better hurry and look around. We'll never get a chance like this again.

THE SECOND WOMAN. (*Crossing to table* D.R.) Just *imagine* who've been in this room! I can almost *feel* the vibrations! To think of you living in Washington and meeting all these people! I wish Henry was a Congressman!

THE FIRST WOMAN. That is her grandfather there. Andrew Chase. My husband says the party's never had a man like him.

THE SECOND WOMAN. Where did he *ever* get that collar?

THE FIRST WOMAN. Isn't it quaint?

THE SECOND WOMAN. My dear, look! (*She heads for a photograph on a table* D.R.) Queen Marie!

THE FIRST WOMAN. (*Joining her.*) Oh!

THE SECOND WOMAN. (*Hands picture to* FIRST WOMAN.) It's *signed!* "Marie R." What's the R. stand for?

FIRST WOMAN. Roumania!

THE SECOND WOMAN. Oh, of course! How silly of me!

(*A frock-coated, foreign-looking man appears in the doorway* D.L. *Caught red-handed, the* TWO WOMEN *affect an elaborate unconcern.*)

THE FOREIGNER. (*With a bow.*) Pardon, Mesdames.

THE FIRST WOMAN. (*Very friendly.*) Howdy do?

SECOND WOMAN. (*Backing toward table.*) Howdy do? (*Putting picture back on table.*)

THE FOREIGNER. (*With a great deal of bowing.*) Pardon. Pardon. (*He withdraws* D.L.)

THE FIRST WOMAN. I think that was the Persian minister. No—Turkish. Anyhow, he is from one of those rug countries.

(SOPHY *appears* D.L. *ushering in a very svelte, beautiful European.*)

THE SECOND WOMAN. (*Crossing over to Stage Center.*) He was awfully foreign, wasn't he?

SOPHY. Come in here, Baroness!

BARONESS. That is so kind of you!

SOPHY. So good of you to come, when you've been so ill. Why don't you sit right down here and I'll have some tea brought in to you?

BARONESS. (*She sits,* L. *Table* D.R.) I'm so sorry to cause you so much trouble!

ORTEGA. (*Speaking on cue* "*been so ill,*" *enters* D.L. *with two other* FOREIGN-LOOKING MEN. *Turning to them.*) Vraiment ça doit être du champagne français, car il est excellent!

SOPHY. (*Crossing to the door* D.L.) Señor Ortega, would you be so good as to ask them to bring the Baroness' tea in here?

ORTEGA. Mais certainement, I will be delighted! (SOPHY *exits* D.L.)

PROTOPOPESCU. Non, non! Permettez-moi! } (*Simulta-*

ORTEGA. Avec plaisir! } *neously.*)

(PROTOPOPESCU *exits* U.C. *and leaves doors open.*)

ORTEGA. (*Crossing to the* BARONESS.) Oh, Baroness— (*As he kisses her hand, there is a smothered squeal from the* CONGRESSMAN'S WIFE *and her* FRIEND.) J'ai été désespéré— J'ai entendu dire que vous avez été malade, mais à vous voir, on ne le croiraix pas.

THE SECOND WOMAN. French!

(*A* CHINESE LADY AND GENTLEMAN *appear in the hallway* U.C.)

BARONESS. Oh—un tout petit malaise que j'ai exagéré pour me rendre plus intéréssante, c'est ce que j'appelle faire Madame au Camelia.

(THREE MEN *grouped around* BARONESS *laugh.*)

ORTEGA. (*Laughing.*) Oh! vous dîtes toujours des choses si drôles, n'est-ce-pas?

CHANG. (*Speaks on entering —crossing to* TWO WOMEN U.L. *In beautiful English, with a bow to the* WOMEN.) If you please. It is, to Mrs. Wayne, this way?

SECOND WOMAN. (*With much nodding and smiling from both* WOMEN.) Yes.

FIRST WOMAN. Yes, that's right.

SECOND WOMAN. Right in there. (CHANG *and his* LADY *start for door* D.L.) Chinese! (*Turning to her* FRIEND.)

ORTEGA. (*Speaking on cue "Chinese".*) Ah! Monsieur Chang!

CHANG. (*About to exit with* HIS LADY, *pauses.*) Ah, c'est un plasir de vous revoir, Monsieur Ortega.

ORTEGA. Je vous remercie, Monsieur Chang!

CHANG. Nous ne nous voyons pas assez souvent. (*Exits* D.L. *with* HIS LADY.)

ORTEGA. Ah! C'est malheureux! (*Turns to the* BARONESS *again.*)

*to a
pleasure
to See you
again*

*We do not
See each
other often enough
Too shame*

THE GENERAL. (*Enters* U.C. *in full uniform*—MRS. DAVENPORT *on his arm*—*Speaks on the first cue, "Monsieur Chang." Leaving doors opened.*) But, of course, Mrs. Davenport, in war as it is fought today all that is taken care of by the tank corps. (*Sees the* BARONESS.) How do you do, Baroness?

BARONESS. Monsieur le général!

GENERAL. (*Starting over* L.) But there is one thing that you must remember: an army travels on its stomach.

MRS. DAVENPORT. Well, isn't that awfully uncomfortable? (*They continue on to door* D.L. PROTOPOPESCU *enters* U.C. *with tea things.*)

GENERAL. (*As they exit* D.L.) No, no, Mrs. Davenport, you don't understand me. What I mean is that an army cannot proceed unless the commissary department, etc.

THE SECOND WOMAN. Sally!

THE FIRST WOMAN. Well?

THE SECOND WOMAN. Remember that napkin I got at the White House?

THE FIRST WOMAN. Yes.

THE SECOND WOMAN. (*Crossing down to desk* L.) Walk in back of me as we go out of here.

(*As they start off the* SECOND WOMAN *deftly picks up an ashtray on the desk and slips it into her handbag. They exit* D.L.)

(ANN *comes in from the hall* U.R. *As she opens the doors there is the usual buzz of conversation from the* GUESTS. *She closes the doors. She brings* LOUELLA MAY CREEVEY, *every inch a club-woman. All blue and gold sash and flowers.*)

ANN. If you'll just come through here, Mrs. Creevey—because this way you can miss all that crowd. If you'll just— Mrs. Wayne has been looking forward to meeting you. (*Closes doors.*)

MRS. CREEVEY. Thank you.

ANN. (*As* MRS. IVES *opportunely enters* D.L. *and crosses to* MRS. CREEVEY, *Center.*) Mary, I want you to meet Mrs. Creevey, President of the Women's Peace,— (*Hesitating.*)

MRS. CREEVEY. (*Prompting her.*) Purity—

ANN. —and Patriotism League. Mrs. Creevey, *will* you excuse me? I just have to run. Mrs. Ives will look after you. Won't you, Mary? (*Exits* U.R. *Closes doors.*)

MRS. IVES. (*You can imagine how pleased.*) Delighted.

MRS. CREEVEY. Mrs. Ives? Mrs. Postmaster-General Ives?

MRS. IVES. That's right.

MRS. CREEVEY. Well, this is wonderful! I'm such an admirer of your husband's, Mrs. Ives. As you may know, I have the honor to represent five million women, including affiliated bodies, and we are not going to rest until we make it ten. And, of course, next year we celebrate our quadri-centennial —doubtless you've read about it—and we have petitioned the Postmaster-General to issue a special stamp in honor of the occasion.

MRS. IVES. I'm sure that would be most appropriate.

MRS. CREEVEY. I'm *so* glad you think so, but the question is: what should be the design on the stamp? The Executive Committee is divided—some think it should be a simple dove of peace, and others think it should be *me*. (*She laughs a little.*) Since the quadri-centennial occurs during my Presidency.

MRS. IVES. I think it would be an excellent idea.

MRS. CREEVEY. I'm so glad you think so. (*She is peering into the other room.*) Oh, isn't that Sir Arthur Erskine?

MRS. IVES. Yes, I think it is.

MRS. CREEVEY. We met at Geneva last spring—the disarmament conference. . . . (HARDWICK *enters* D.L.) And here's Senator Hardwick! How fortunate! I was looking for you at the Capitol all morning.

HARDWICK. Yes, ma'am. I heard you were. (*Clipping cigar tip.*)

MRS. IVES. Well, pardon me. I'll tell Mrs. Wayne you're here. (SHE *escapes, crossing below* HARDWICK *to door* D.L. *and exits.*)

MRS. CREEVEY. (*As* HARDWICK *starts to go* MRS. CREEVEY *stops him.*) (*Abstracted.*) What? Oh, yes. Now, Senator, as you know I represent six million women in forty-seven of the forty-eight States. Your own State has one of our *strongest* chapters, and we do *so* much want to support you in your campaign for re-election this Fall—

HARDWICK. Well, that's very good of you.

MRS. CREEVEY. —if we can feel sure just how you stand. The question is: Whom are you going to nominate for President? We want a man who had a mother, Senator Hardwick. The women of America, Senator—

(LUCY, *having been duly tipped off, swoops down on* MRS. CREEVEY *from the other room*, D.L.)

LUCY. Mrs. Creevey! Hello, Tom!

HARDWICK. Hello, Lucy!

LUCY. So *nice* of you to come! (HARDWICK *takes advantage of the distraction and tiptoes down left and exits.*) With all the *terrific* responsibilities that you have— (SOPHY *enters* D.L. *with* MRS. CREEVEY'S *corsage of gardenias for* LUCY) and this *marvelous* convention! I hear it's the most inspiring one you've ever had! (SOPHY, *back of* LUCY, *deftly slips the corsage to* LUCY.) And to *think* of you sending me these beautiful flowers! (SOPHY *exits* D.L.)

MRS. CREEVEY. I've just been telling the Senator (*Looks around for* HARDWICK, *who has gone*)—where did the Senator go? Oh, well, I've just been telling the Senator that we

must have a President that the six million women of the
W.P.P.P. can get behind.

LUCY. Well, of course that takes a big man.

MRS. CREEVEY. Indeed it does, Mrs. Wayne. The women of
America *demand* such a man. The hand that rocks the
cradle must also be the mailed fist. Don't you agree with
me?

LUCY. Oh, absolutely! And now I want everyone to meet
you! Baroness, may I present Mrs. Creevey? Mrs. Creevey
is behind six million women.

MRS. CREEVEY. No, no. They're behind *me*.

LUCY. (*Crossing over to* BARONESS' *group.*) I beg your pardon. This is the Baroness Orloff, Señor Ortega, M. Pavitch
—ah, M. Protopopescu! Quand êtes-vous rentré de New
York?

PROTOPOPESCU. Avant-hier.

LUCY. Baroness, c'est gentil d'être venue, madame! Mais la-
jolie robe! Elle vous va à ravir!

BARONESS. Merci, merci!

LUCY. And now, Mrs. Creevey, everyone is *dying* to meet
you! (*She starts off with* MRS. CREEVEY, D.L.) Mrs. Creevey,
I don't see how you do it! All those women behind you!
What do they *do* back there, anyhow? (LUCY *and* MRS.
CREEVEY *exit to Drawing-room* D.L.)

(*Meanwhile the* BARONESS *and* HER GROUP *are wending their
way toward the hall, jabbering French as they go.*)

ORTEGA. (*Looking at his watch.*) Ah, mon Dieu! Il fait
tard, et j'ai un rendezvous à l'ambassade.

BARONESS. (*Rising and handing tea-cup to* M. PAVITCH,
starts with HER GROUP U.C.) A propos, Monsieur Ortega,
que pensez-vous de la note de Mussolini?

ORTEGA. Cela depend—nous ne marchons que de surprises en surprises.

(*As they pass through the hall doors a* NEWCOMER *enters.* FOREIGN GROUP *bows to him and exits* U.C. *The* NEWCOMER *is* GORDON KEANE. *He is a good-looking man, tall, well set-up. He comes into the room rather uncertainly—plainly, he is a stranger.*)

(*The* GENERAL *comes back* D.L. *again with* MRS. DAVENPORT.)

THE GENERAL. In my opinion, Mrs. Davenport, in my opinion, war with Japan is inevitable!

MRS. DAVENPORT. Really? Will you bring me back a kimono?

(KEANE *enters* U.C.)

THE GENERAL. Certainly! I'll have the Mikado help me pick it out.

MRS. DAVENPORT. That'll be fine. When will I get it?

THE GENERAL. Why, I'll start the war right away, Mrs. Davenport. (*To* KEANE.) Senator— (*Starts* U.C.) What size do you wear, if I'm not being too personal? (*As they exit* U.C.)

(GORDON KEANE *peers into the drawing-room, seems a little hesitant about entering.*) (EMMY *comes out of the room* D.L.)

EMMY. (*Crossing to* KEANE.) Oh! You're Senator Keane!

KEANE. How do you do?

EMMY. I'm Emmy Paige, Mrs. Wayne's niece. I've seen you in the Senate—that's how I happened to know you.

KEANE. You have a good memory. There are a lot of us up there!

EMMY. Well, I'd know you anywhere by the top of your head. Of course, sitting in the gallery and looking down on you you look kind of different, but I couldn't mistake you. You're the only one that's got that much hair!

KEANE. Well, I'm glad I stand out some way. . . . Tell me —where do I find Mrs. Wayne? In there? Or is this the wrong end to begin at?

EMMY. Well, I know Aunt Lucy wants to see you. I'll try to get her!

KEANE. Thanks. I don't know whether I'm quite equal to plunging into that.

EMMY. That's all right. (*She goes,* D.L. *Alone again,* KEANE *gives his attention to the room. Its chief attraction for him is the portrait of Andrew Chase.* EMMY *returns, bringing* LUCY, *true to her word.*) I got her.

LUCY. (*Crossing to* KEANE.) So you made it! (*They shake hands.*)

KEANE. Indeed I did. We adjourned early.

LUCY. Well, I thought the speech came off awfully well, didn't you? I heard several very nice things about it.

KEANE. I'm glad of that. But I'm afraid the whole thing was your doing, more than mine.

LUCY. Nonsense! What did I do? A little adding and sub-tracting. . . . Emmy, tell Charles to bring us some tea in here. And if Belle or Mary Ives gets a minute off tell them to come in.

EMMY. Yes, Aunt Lucy.

LUCY. (*Crosses table* D.R.) And oh, Emmy! See if your *Uncle* Stephen's downstairs. (*As* EMMY *goes,* D.L.) He's probably up to his shoulder-blades in peace women, but I want you two to have a talk. I know you'll like each other. (*Sits R. of table.*)

KEANE. I'm looking forward to it. You understand, Mrs. Wayne, I admire the Secretary very much, even if I don't always see eye to eye with him.

LUCY. Well, anyhow, I want you to hear his views. Do sit down. (KEANE *sits.*) We can have a nice long talk after all this crowd goes. Of course it's rather hectic now.

KEANE. (*Looking around.*) You know, this is an event for me—sitting in this room. (*Looking at the portrait.*) He was a wonderful-looking man, wasn't he? Your grandfather's always been a sort of ideal of mine.

LUCY. Oh, I'm glad.

(*Enter* D.L. 2ND BUTLER *and* CHARLES *carrying tray of crumpets and tea-tray. Cross to table* D.R.)

KEANE. Of course, I was only a boy when he was President—my father took me to hear him speak once. I couldn't have been more than seven. His train came through the town and he spoke from the back platform. I'll never forget it.

LUCY. I've got some wonderful pictures of those old campaigns—they're lots of fun. . . . Oh, thank you, Charles. (*The tea tray is set down.*) (2ND BUTLER *and* CHARLES *exit* D.L.) I'll show them to you later on. . . . Tea?

KEANE. Yes, thanks, plain. . . . I suppose he must have sat here hundreds of times. Your grandfather.

LUCY. Well, of course he liked Blue Hills best. I can't remember when we didn't live with him,—either at Blue Hills, or Gramercy Park, or the Governor's mansion.

KEANE. It must have been a great experience. And how he must have loved *you.*

LUCY. Well, my father was his only child, you know, and he adored my mother. Of course, I ate it up—there was always something exciting going on. But it had its drawbacks—I was patted on the head by practically every member of the party. Maybe that's what's the matter with me.

HARDWICK. (*Entering.*) Hello, Keane. How are you?

KEANE. (*Rises—he shakes hands, tea-cup in hand.*) Hello, Senator.

LUCY. (*Rises. Crosses to* C., *stands between* HARDWICK *and* KEANE, *as she talks first to one, then the other.*) Tom here was one of the chief head-patters—I was just talking about old times. You know, during his second term grandfather had the most wonderful cabinet. They were the best poker players in America.

HARDWICK. Those were the days, all right—the golden days of American politics.

LUCY. Mm. The chewing-tobacco era. I'll never forget Vice-President Merritt—remember, Tom?—when he congratulated mother on having the couch just the right spitting distance from the fire-place. Of course mother had a sort of sixth sense about spittoons. It was part of her success in the White House.

(MRS. IVES *enters, not a little disturbed.*)

MRS. IVES. Well, I put my foot in it with Mrs. Creevey. I admired a sweet little flower nestling in her jabot, and she said, "Flower? What flower?" Well, my dear, it turned out to be a little dab of chicken salad, with mayonnaise on it.

(BELLE HARDWICK *comes in,* D.L.)

BELLE. (*Crossing to table* D.R.) Well, this is peaceful.

LUCY. Want a cup of tea, Belle? (*Sits* R. *of table.*)

BELLE. I certainly do. (*She sinks into a chair, L. of table.*) (LUCY *hands cup of tea to* BELLE.) Whew! My poor feet! I've spent the whole afternoon walking around on broken English.

(SOPHY *enters* U.L.—*a bit apprehensively. Crosses down to* LUCY.)

LUCY. Belle, you know Senator Keane, Mrs. Hardwick?

KEANE. Oh, yes. How do you do, Mrs. Hardwick? (*Hands tea to* BELLE.)

BELLE. How are you, Senator?

LUCY. Well, Sophy? Is Rome still burning while we're fiddling?

SOPHY. Lucy! (*She advances and whispers to her.*)

LUCY. (*Vastly amused.*) Not really? Here?

SOPHY. Very much here. Ann Forrester has her in tow.

LUCY. (*Rises and crosses below table.*) Oh, she must come right in! Where is she?

ANN. Right in here, Mrs. Hibbard. (TOM *rises—leans against desk. There is a moment's pause, and then* IRENE HIBBARD *enters* U.R. *Born Irene Baker in Mansfield, Ohio, but Europe was her finishing school. She can only be described in French. Elégante, soignée, chic.* BELLE *rises.* KEANE *puts cup on mantel.*)

LUCY. (*Crossing up to* IRENE.) Irene! How like you to give us this pleasure!

IRENE. I'm sorry to be so late. But I had no idea I could make it.

LUCY. Neither had I.

IRENE. (*Taking in the assemblage.*) I know everyone, don't I? Yes.

BELLE. (*Crossing to R. below table.*) You know me.

IRENE. Oh, hello, Belle. Mary!—Tom, darling! (*Her whole tone is different when she addresses a man.*) I don't see you nearly often enough.

HARDWICK. (*The gay old dog.*) Just give me a chance, Irene.

IRENE. (*Turning aside the compliment.*) Oh, Tom! . . . And Gordon! Well! To think of finding *you* here!

LUCY. Yes, think of that.

KEANE. Mrs. Wayne was so kind as to invite me.

IRENE. How sweet of her!

LUCY. (*Sits R. of table.*) Won't you sit down, Irene? You look tired.

IRENE. (*Sits R. of table.*) Thank you. (*As she settles herself her bag slips to the floor.* GORDON *bounds after it.* BELLE *sits in chair R. of fireplace.*) Oh, thanks, Gordon. . . . You're looking—better, Lucy.

LUCY. Only two pounds better.

IRENE. But it's becoming.

LUCY. Thank you.

IRENE. (*Extracting a cigarette from a dainty case.*) Have you a light, Gordon? (*He quickly strikes a match.*) Oh, thank you. . . . You know, I've been telling Gordon for weeks that he ought to come here once. I knew he'd enjoy it.

LUCY. Oh, I hope you didn't force the poor man, Irene. . . . Tea?

IRENE. If you please.

LUCY. You take a—?

IRENE. Lemon.

LUCY. Lemon, oh, yes. Crumpets?

IRENE. Thank you.

LUCY. Of course, they're nothing compared to those *your* chef makes. (*She turns to* KEANE.) Irene has the most wonderful chef, Gordon. You must go *there* to tea sometime. . . . Once. (BELLE'S *cup descends on its saucer with a sudden and audible click. There is a moment's hiatus, devoted to tea-drinking and general uneasiness.*) Well, this is cozy, isn't it? (*She takes out a cigarette; parrots* IRENE'S *inflection.*) Have you a light, Gordon? (*There is a flicker from* IRENE *as* GORDON *lights* LUCY'S *cigarette.*)

HARDWICK. Nobody asks *me* for a light. I've got a lighter, too. (*He exhibits it and works it.*)

IRENE. Really, it must be frightful for you to have to do this sort of thing, Lucy—these terrible crowds. People who don't care anything about you, nor you about them. Politics would simply kill me. But then, I'm too sincere.

LUCY. *You* seem to be taking an interest in politics lately, Irene. I saw you lunching with old Senator Taylor today—you were having a wonderful time.

IRENE. Oh, were you there?

LUCY. And Senator Taylor, too—I never saw him so captivated. How I envy you your knack with older men. (IRENE'S *silence is eloquent.*) That reminds me, how's your husband? He didn't come with you, did he?

IRENE. No, Carter's busy. He's writing a minority opinion.

LUCY. Again? I'm so sorry.

IRENE. Well, at least Carter can afford to express an opinion. The bench is permanent.

LUCY. Yes, it must give you such a comfortable feeling, like royalty, almost. But you *were*, almost, weren't you? Of course! What was that fascinating little country you lived in?

IRENE. If you mean Prince Gregoravitch's country, it was Slovania.

LUCY. Oh, yes. Slovania! (*Addressing this mainly to* KEANE.) She had the most beautiful crest—a gorgeous crown, and unicorns sitting on sweet-breads, or something —that's one thing you got out of it, anyhow, Irene. That crest. I remember when you had the place at Middleburg, how beautiful it looked on the bed linen! Of course it left welts on the funniest places.

(STEPHEN WAYNE *comes in,* D.L.)

STEPHEN. Well! So this is where you all are? Hello, Tom! Mary! Ann! And Irene! Well! (*Crossing to* IRENE.)

IRENE. Stephen! (*An impulsive arm stretches out to greet him.*) You know, you're getting handsomer every day.

STEPHEN. Well, you *couldn't* be more handsome.

IRENE. (*Really, she didn't expect* that.) Stephen!

STEPHEN. Hello, Senator, glad to see you.

KEANE. Mr. Secretary.

STEPHEN. Mrs. Wayne tells me you made a very fine speech this afternoon, Senator. I'd like to read it.

KEANE. Oh, thanks.

LUCY. Yes, it was really superb. I was so glad I happened to be there to hear it.

IRENE. Yes, you *were* lucky, weren't you?

LUCY. Wasn't I? I don't know how I happened to drop in just today. Intuition, I guess.

IRENE. Almost psychic, wasn't it? . . . I should think Stephen could make use of such a gift—a clairvoyant in the family.

STEPHEN. (*Crossing to L. to* MRS. IVES.) You mustn't take it too seriously, Irene. It's just the gypsy in her.

LUCY. Thank you, dear.

IRENE. (*Rises.*) Well, Gordon and I have got to be going. We're driving over into Maryland—to the Hendricks'.

LUCY. Oh!

IRENE. Come, Gordon.

KEANE. I—I didn't have a chance to tell you. (*To* IRENE, U.C.) There's plenty of time, isn't there?

IRENE. I'm afraid not. You know, Senator Hendricks wants to talk to you before the others get there. (*She turns to the rest of the room.*) It's rather important. (*To* LUCY.)

LUCY. (*Rises.*) Oh, then, you'd better start *now*, Gordon. Because sometimes Irene's car breaks down.

IRENE. (*Ignoring this.*) Are you ready, Gordon?

KEANE. (*None too comfortable.*) Yes, if you think we— Mrs. Wayne (*turns to* LUCY) was going to show me some old photographs.

IRENE. Not really? Dragging out the memoirs again, Lucy? "My Life and Times in the White House." Oh, you can see those any time—can't he, Lucy? They're *always* on exhibition.

KEANE. Well—then if I may come again . . .

LUCY. May he, Irene?

IRENE. Of course!

LUCY. Thank you!

IRENE. I wouldn't dream of his missing those photographs! With you in bloomers, playing basketball, or riding piggy-back on dear old Grandpa! . . . Well, good-bye, every-body! We just *must* run! Good-bye, Lucy!

LUCY. Good-bye!

IRENE. You're so fortunate to have a past, my dear. It gives you something to talk about. Come, Gordon, we simply must run. We're very late!

(*She sweeps out, taking* KEANE *with her. He mumbles a "Good-bye, Mrs. Wayne," as he disappears* U.R.) (SOPHY *follows her out* U.R.—*She closes the doors.*) (LUCY *leans against the table.*)

BELLE. Count ten, Lucy. Count ten before you say a word.

STEPHEN. (*Quietly.*) Well, I got here a little late, but as an old State Department man I gather that the situation is a bit strained.

HARDWICK. (*Crosses to* R.) Tough luck, Lucy. I thought you had her going for a while there.

STEPHEN. Well, suppose we leave the girls to mop up. A battlefield's no place for a diplomat, eh, Tom?

HARDWICK. I would have put two to one on you, Lucy. Something's happened to your footwork. (*Leaves doors open.*)

STEPHEN. (*Starts* U.C.) We'll be upstairs, Lucy, if she comes back with reinforcements.

(BELLE *puts cup on mantel.*) (*The* MEN *go out* U.L.)
(STEPHEN *closes the doors.*)

MRS. IVES. (*Crossing to* R.) Well, I never saw such a thing
in all my life. The effrontery!

LUCY. It *was* good, wasn't it?

ANN. Well, I guess we ought to go back to work, shouldn't
we?

MRS. IVES. Oh, all right. (*Looks off* L.) Though I should
think those women would be waterlogged, from the tea
they've put away.

ANN. (*Starting for* D.L. *door.*) Yes, how do they stand it?
An eternal diet of party food.

MRS. IVES. (*Following* ANN.) But they do it. Look at the
Vice-President's wife. Why, she can lick her weight in let-
tuce sandwiches.

(MRS. IVES *and* ANN *pass into the drawing-room* D.L.)

LUCY. (*Who has been holding it in all this time.*) Piggy-
back! Did you hear that? (BELLE *crosses to table.*) What
about *her* picture in one of those Baker Steamers that but-
toned up the back! The nerve of her!

(BELLE *crosses to her.*)

BELLE. Well, what did you expect?

LUCY. (*Pacing.*) But in my own house, Belle! She came
right into my own house and *took* him! As if he were flat
silver!

(WARN DINING-ROOM LIGHT.)

BELLE. You're not surprised, are you? The years you've
been in this town—*you* ought to be able to guess what's
back of it?

LUCY. Back of it?

BELLE. Don't you know what year this is, Lucy?

LUCY. What do you mean?

BELLE. This is a Presidential year.

LUCY. Presidential? Keane! . . . But where does Irene come in? What's *she* got to do with it?

BELLE. Everything. That Western crowd will jump through hoops for her. I tell you I know what I'm talking about. She's steering him for the White House.

LUCY. Keane in the White House? But I still don't—what would Irene get out of it?

BELLE. Only—First Lady.

LUCY. (*Crossing to* R. *below* BELLE.) You're out of your mind, Belle.

BELLE. Am I? Think a minute. She's through with Carter Hibbard—you know that. This is her big chance. Keane is younger, and attractive, and it just *may* happen that he gets it. You know politics.

LUCY. But *Irene*, Belle! Irene in the White House! It's too funny.

BELLE. Nothing is too funny for this town. And Keane is just the kind they might fall for. Good-looking, Western, and doesn't know a thing. Am I right or wrong?

(SOPHY *returns* U.L.) (LIGHTS *Dining-room Up.*) (*After she closes doors.*)   (WARN CURTAIN.)

SOPHY. Oh, *this* is where you are. Well, I can't say that I blame you.

BELLE. (*Moving away.*) Anyhow, pleasant dreams, Lucy. (*Starts off.*) I'll see what the girls in the back room will have. (*Exits* D.L.)

SOPHY. Don't you think you'd better go in, Lucy? They're breaking up.

LUCY. So am I. *Sit*

SOPHY. What?

LUCY. (*Pacing up and down.*) (*Half to herself.*) I knew there was something behind it. I knew it.

SOPHY. What? What are you talking about?

LUCY. And it's so simple when you really get hold of it. She's going to divorce Carter, and marry Keane, and make him President. Just like that.

SOPHY. I wish you'd talk English, Lucy.

LUCY. Only I'm not going to let her, Sophy. Keane in the White House when they could have a man like Stephen! Why doesn't she mind her own business, anyhow? What if she is sick of Carter Hibbard and that Supreme Court black night-gown of his? When I think of Stephen— (*She stops suddenly as she slowly gets an idea.*) Sophy!

SOPHY. What?

LUCY. Sophy!

SOPHY. What is it?

LUCY. Sophy!

SOPHY. If you say that again, Lucy—

LUCY. (C.) Sophy, if she thought Carter had a chance to be President—a bigger chance than Keane, Sophy—what would she do? She'd stick to him, wouldn't she? You bet she would!

SOPHY. I suppose so, but—

LUCY. So what we've got to do, Sophy, is make Irene think her husband's *going* to be President! We're going to launch a Presidential boom. For Carter Hibbard! Get it, Sophy?

SOPHY. But they'd never *think* of picking Carter!

LUCY. Of course they wouldn't—that's the whole point. But we've got to make Irene *think* they would. (*Crosses to* R. *below table.*)

SOPHY. Lucy—

LUCY (*Coming back to* SOPHY.) Just a little bit of a boom, Sophy—just big enough to make Irene stay with Carter— happily with Carter. And incidentally sidetrack Gordon Keane. . . . Piggy-back, eh? Well, she'll wish *she* was a piggy-back before I get through with her!

SOPHY. Lucy, you're out of your mind!

LUCY. The only question is: How are we going to go about it? How do you launch a Presidential boom? Sophy? How do you launch a Presidential boom?

MRS. CREEVEY. (*Heard off-stage.*) Thank you, my dear! (MRS. CREEVEY *enters* D.L., *followed by* EMMY.) Oh, here you are, Mrs. Wayne!

LUCY. (*As she puts two and two together.*) Mrs. Creevey!

MRS. CREEVEY. (*Crossing to* LUCY.) I'm so sorry I have to rush. You see, ex-officio I am a member of every committee, and—

LUCY. My dear Mrs. Creevey, I'm so sorry I didn't get a real chance to talk to you—why don't you have lunch with me here tomorrow, just we two?

MRS. CREEVEY. Why, Mrs. Wayne, I'd be delighted.

LUCY. Oh, that'll be fine! Just the two of us and not *any* affiliated bodies! Because I know just the man for you to get behind!

MRS. CREEVEY. Really, Mrs. Wayne?

LUCY. The *very* man! You see, you'll get behind *him* and then *I'll* get behind you—Sophy will get behind us— (*She is suiting the action to the word.*) Why, the possibilities (*They start* U.C.) are endless! (CURTAIN STARTS DOWN.) (*The* BUTLERS *open the dining-room door; a babble of conversation is heard from the* GUESTS *grouped around the dining-room table.*) Shall we say one o'clock? Or if you'd prefer, one-fifteen, Mrs. Creevey! One-twenty, one-twenty-five. . . .

MEDIUM CURTAIN

ACT II

Scene I

SCENE: *Carter Hibbard's study.*

This is a small room—perhaps oval in shape. Walls lined with bookcases filled with books that are obviously "in re" or "vs." something. Law reports, reference works, etc. Classical busts on top of bookcases, and, by way of contrast, a great mounted fish—a particularly homely fish, so realistically stuffed that you can almost hear it gasp. All of the furniture is heavy, ponderous. A Supreme Court chamber in miniature.

In the biggest of the chairs, left, sits CARTER HIBBARD, *Associate Justice of the Supreme Court. In his sixties—dignified, solemn. A pile of law journals and Congressional Records at his elbow.*

He looks at his watch; makes a little rumbling sound and pats his stomach. Adjusts his glasses.

At the other side of the room IRENE HIBBARD *sits regarding him. Resplendent in evening clothes, obviously not donned just to sit home with Carter Hibbard. Jeweled sandals reveal toes.*

A BUTLER, BLEECKER *by name, is discovered on, pouring a cup of coffee for* IRENE.

(WARN RADIO.)

BLEECKER. (*Leaves coffee pot on table and then goes to* HIBBARD.) Your Sanka, sir. (*Puts it on the desk.*)

52

HIBBARD. Ah—my soda tablets. I don't see my soda tablets.

BLEECKER. (*Gets them on desk behind inkstand.*) Right here, sir. (*Gives them to* HIBBARD *and exits with his tray* U.C.)

HIBBARD. Oh, yes, yes.

(*He looks at his watch. Switches on the knob of a radio that stands near him. The music of a dance orchestra comes over the air. Takes a cigar from the humidor on the desk. Pulls out an elaborate bunch of gadgets on a heavy chain and fumbles for a cigar clipper. Clips the cigar and lights it. He reaches for his newspaper. Shakes it out and settles to his reading.*)   (RADIO SOFT.)

IRENE, *plainly, is in a mood. Each of these little separate acts of* CARTER'S *has brought her nearer to the breaking-point. Toes tap the floor; she gulps down her demi-tasse at one swallow.*)

IRENE (*When* CARTER *has finally settled himself.*) I never saw a room with so many books in it and nothing to read! "In re" and "versus" and the State of Michigan! Or *this!* (*She picks up a brilliantly-colored detective story.*) "Murder in a Phone Booth." Oh, I know, I know. It relaxes you.

HIBBARD. (*Rises.*) I'm sorry, my dear. (*He starts to give her half the newspaper.*)

IRENE. I don't want the paper.
(HIBBARD *sits down again. There is another pause as he absorbs himself in his reading.*)

HIBBARD. (*Laughing aloud.*) Ah, Snooky-Wookums and her pals are very amusing this evening. You see, yesterday Snooky-Wookums poured a whole bucket of quicklime over Dimple-Face—that's a little friend of hers—and to-day Dimple-Face contrives to have Snooky-Wookums carried off in a garbage wagon. (*He laughs again.*) I don't see how these fellows think of something new every day.

IRENE. (*Whose eyes have been elsewhere.*) Carter!

HIBBARD. Yes, my dear?

IRENE. Would you mind terribly if I did something about that fish?

HIBBARD. What?

IRENE. If I could just get it to close its mouth.

HIBBARD. My dear, that is one of the finest specimens of American amberjack. I caught that off the Florida Coast—

IRENE. (*Mechanically.*) On February 26th, nineteen hundred and seventeen. It weighs twenty-seven pounds and measures three feet four and a half inches to the tip of the tail.

HIBBARD. Really, my dear—your tone!

(WARN STATIC RADIO.)

IRENE. It was the year we were married—nineteen seventeen.

HIBBARD. Ah! Then that's how you remember.

IRENE. Yes. That's how. (*Her eyes go to the wall again.*) We were caught the same year.

(*Before* CARTER *can frame an answer to this,* BLEECKER *has entered with brandy glass on tray for* HIBBARD; *places it on desk, puts the cup on the tray.*)

HIBBARD. Ah—Bleecker.

BLEECKER. Yes, sir?

HIBBARD. My Ovaltine was not hot last night. I wish you'd always have it very hot.

BLEECKER. I'm sorry, sir.

HIBBARD. (*Looking at his watch.*) What time do you have, Bleecker?

BLEECKER. Five minutes to eight, sir.

HIBBARD. Yes, that agrees with mine. (BLEECKER *starts off.*) (*He fools with the dial a little; there is a burst of static, then music again.*)   (MUSIC STATIC.)

IRENE. Bleecker!

BLEECKER. Yes, madam?

IRENE. Will you let me know as soon as the car is here?

BLEECKER. Yes, madam.

IRENE. And if Senator Keane telephones tell him I'm stopping at the Racquet Club for him.

BLEECKER. Yes, madam. (*He exits* U.C.)

HIBBARD. Aren't you going out a great deal lately, my dear?

IRENE. What should I do? Stay home?

HIBBARD. I do not consider that a becoming response to a courteous question. Besides, you know George Mason is coming here tonight.

IRENE. George Mason! Why should I stay in to see George Mason?

HIBBARD. Well, he seemed to make a point of it. I can't imagine what his errand is—he was very mysterious about it.

IRENE. Probably wants to tell you about a fish he caught. . . . I'm sorry, Carter, but I've made other plans.

HIBBARD. All right, my dear.

(IRENE *pours another cup of coffee.*)

                (WARN RADIO, SWELL, SOFT.)

HIBBARD. Two cups of coffee? It'll keep you awake.

IRENE. I hope to ~~God~~ *Heaven* it does. Until the car comes.

(*The* HIBBARD *stomach gives another premonitory rumble.*)

HIBBARD. My stomach seems to be getting worse and worse.

IRENE. Well, you will race through your dinner, and make me race through mine. All to get to your radio by eight o'clock.

HIBBARD. Surely, my dear, you do not expect me to miss the Whoops Family.

IRENE. Seven o'clock! No civilized person dines at seven o'clock! And it completely spoils the servants.

HIBBARD. It is not early dining that has given me my bad stomach. It's the rich food prepared by that colored chef of yours. I'll never be any better till you get rid of him.

IRENE. Carter, we've been over this a thousand times. He'd go straight back to Lucy Wayne, and I'm not going to let her have him.

HIBBARD. (*Dial bus.*) That's the real trouble with my stomach. Fried chicken, not the Whoops Family. I shouldn't eat *anything* fried! (*Fools again with the dial.*)

                (START MUSIC)

IRENE. Carter.   (SWELL MUSIC.)

HIBBARD. H'm?

IRENE. (*Shouting above din of the radio.*) I'm going to Middleburg over the week-end. The Anthonys.

HIBBARD. What?   (SOFT.)

IRENE. (*Still shouting, although* CARTER *has toned down the radio.*) I'm going to spend the week-end with the Anthonys. In Middleburg.   (WARN RADIO.)

HIBBARD. (*He looks up.*) *This* week-end? Saturday is the Chief Justice's dinner.

IRENE. Well, what *of* it?

HIBBARD. What of it? We must go there together. There are two places that we must always go together—the Chief Justice's and the White House.

IRENE. The Chief Justice's dinners bore me to death. Habeas corpus, and you're home again at ten-thirty. And the Anthonys are having a very amusing crowd.

HIBBARD. That's beside the point. The Chief Justice is the Chief Justice. (*Looks at his newspaper.*) (*Suddenly he is reminded of an amusing incident in the day's work.*) He was very perturbed today. You should have been there. Henshaw contended that a judgment resting on service by publication was not valid as a judgment in persona. A most interesting case. I brought the briefs home with me. (*At desk.*) Now, where are those papers? (*He is looking around, seeking papers on his desk.*)

IRENE. (*Quite calmly.*) I ate them.

HIBBARD. How's that?

IRENE. I ate them.   (DIM MUSIC.)

HIBBARD. My dear, you're behaving very peculiarly to-night.

(*The radio interrupts.*)   (STOP MUSIC, VOICE.)

THE RADIO. Station JDK, Washington.

HIBBARD. Ah, here we are!

THE RADIO. The correct time is fifteen seconds after eight o'clock.   (RADIO.)

HIBBARD. (*Looking at his watch.*) I have just ten.

RADIO. The J. K. Starrett Corporation presents The Whoops
Family.   (SWELL MUSIC.)

IRENE. (*As the Whoops Family theme song is softly played
over the radio, rises.*) Carter, will you turn that off, please?
(*Crosses to* R.)

HIBBARD. (*As he dials down.*) Turn it off? Irene, you know
very well that after the grind of the day's work the clean
wholesome fun of the Whoops Family—

IRENE. Relaxes you! I know! And when you're relaxed you
stay relaxed until Bleecker brings your Ovaltine, and that
relaxes you *again!* And then you go to bed, and GOD! how
you relax!

HIBBARD. That is an unreasonable contention, my dear. The
greatest minds in history required relaxation. Take Abraham
Lincoln. He too relished an occasional bit of humor.

IRENE. Yes, Carter. But you have all of Lincoln's annoying
qualities and none of his great ones.

HIBBARD. (*Aghast.*) Really, my dear!   (VOICE.)

THE RADIO. Good evening, folks! What is it that gives that
lovely, sweet taste to the mouth when little tousle-heads
make ready for another day? It is Dr. Mackintosh's
Sweetie-Wheaties, especially prepared for the—

(IRENE, *in a fury, strides to the radio and snaps it off.*)

                     (STOP VOICE, MUSIC.)

HIBBARD (*Rises.*) (*On his feet.*) Irene!

IRENE. I'm through, Carter.

HIBBARD. What's that?

IRENE. I'm through. Through, done, finished!

HIBBARD. My dear, this is a most unseemly exhibition.

IRENE. Oh, come down off that bench! Stop being a Supreme Court judge and be a human being just long enough to *understand* this. I'm leaving you, Carter. I'm leaving you because I can't stand it—*one—minute—longer.*

HIBBARD. You don't know what you're saying! Because I turned on the radio?

IRENE. (*In an unnatural voice.*) Yes! Because you turned on the radio. That's as good a reason as any.

HIBBARD. But that's absurd. That wouldn't stand in a court of law.

IRENE. (*Pacing.*) Law, law! What's law got to do with marriage? What's law compared to the Whoops Family, and those briefs you bring home, and that fish up on the wall, and that kit of tools that you carry in your pocket, and your stomach, stomach, stomach! What's law got to do with your stomach! Answer me that!

HIBBARD. So! This is a case of incompatibility!

IRENE. And sitting here night after night! Night after night after night after night after night! Relaxing!

HIBBARD. (*Finally stung.*) You haven't sat here very many nights. Traipsing around with young Keane all over the place! How about *that?*

IRENE. Well, Senator Keane—!

HIBBARD. Is it my stomach or Senator Keane that's at the root of this? I suppose he hasn't *got* a stomach!

IRENE. I never should have married a man so much older.

HIBBARD. (*Crossing to her.*) You're not so young any more. You haven't been able to look up a telephone number for five years!

IRENE. Leave my age out of this!

HIBBARD. You tried marrying a younger man. That didn't work so well either.

IRENE. Leave my marriage out of it, too!

HIBBARD. You bought your rotten little Prince Gregoravitch and then you had to buy the filthy Slovanian courts to get rid of him—when I think of myself mixing in that mess! You were just as eager then for respectability and security as you are now to escape from them! Well, I've given them to you! The daughter of Sockless Sam Baker is the wife of a Supreme Court Justice!

IRENE. You leave my father out of this!

HIBBARD. Sockless Sam Baker! Never took a spoon out of a coffee cup! And I've given you a social position second to none! (*He crosses back to the desk.*)

IRENE. Thank you so much. It's so courteous of you to remind me. And I suppose I didn't *buy you,* too, as you so delicately put it? All those years when you were counsel for Baker Steamers. Doing *their* dirty work!

HIBBARD. Irene, you know my stomach. You know what those scenes do to me, a man with my constitution. (*Sinks in the desk chair.*)

IRENE. (*Crossing to him.*) Constitution! If it isn't *your* constitution it's the country's—I don't know which is the more deadly! All I know is that I'm sick of them both! I'm sick of *you,* if you must know! And you don't want me! You've got your Supreme Court and your fish—that's all you care about! Just be careful that you don't get them mixed up! (*Crosses to* R.)

HIBBARD. (*Rises.*) That will do, Irene. You have chosen to cast aspersion upon my calling—the highest and noblest in

all the world. It is an offense I can neither forgive nor
condone.

IRENE. (*Crosses to* C.) That suits me, as long as you understand the situation. I want a divorce and I want it quickly.
You got me one when you were a dinkey Cleveland lawyer;
it ought to be easy for a Supreme Court Judge.

HIBBARD. You'll get your divorce— Go! And take that fancy
chef with you. No one will reproach *me;* before the bar of
public opinion, the onus will be borne by you. (*A step to
her.*)

IRENE. Onus! Onus! Do you think anyone cares what the
wife of a Supreme Court Judge does? Do you think anyone
even knows that a Supreme Court Judge has a wife? Do
you suppose a Supreme Court Justice is credited with any
passion stronger than *heartburn!*

HIBBARD. (*With enormous dignity.*) The discussion is at an
end.

(*As if to emphasize this, he starts to turn the radio knob.
There is a knock on the door.* BLEECKER *enters.*)

BLEECKER. Judge Mason is here, sir.

HIBBARD. What? Oh, yes, yes, yes. Bring him in.

IRENE. (*Hastily collecting her accessories.*) I'm getting out
of here!

(*Before she can escape, however,* MASON'S VOICE *is heard in
the hallway. She is trapped.*)

MASON. Thank you, Bleecker. Here you are, Mrs. Creevey.

(MRS. CREEVEY—LOUELLA MAY CREEVEY—*looms up in the
doorway, and with her* JUDGE MASON. *A pleasant-looking
man, somewhere in his fifties. Behind the two of them, not
visible for a moment, is a gentleman of decided presence.*

It is only by reason of his being a stranger in the house that he is not in charge of the little flock. His name is GANNING— ELLSWORTH T. GANNING.)

MASON. (*Crossing down, shakes hands.*) Good evening, Carter! Irene! Mr. Justice, I've taken the liberty of bringing along some mighty fine folks—two people that are among your greatest admirers. Irene, I want to introduce you to Mrs. Creevey—

MRS. CREEVEY. Mrs. Louella May Creevey, president of the Women's Peace, Purity and Patriotism League. It is indeed a pleasure, Mrs. Hibbard.

MASON. And Mr. Justice Hibbard.

MRS. CREEVEY. Mr. Justice! What an honor!

HIBBARD. (*Crosses to her.*) Very kind of you, I'm sure.

MASON. And this man you don't have to be introduced to. Ellsworth T. Ganning, of the Ganning newspapers.

GANNING. Mrs. Hibbard.

HIBBARD. How do you do, sir?

GANNING. (*Crosses to* HIBBARD.) Mr. Justice, this is an occasion that has been too long deferred. Our mutual friend Harper Knowles was to have brought us together in December, but at the last minute I had to address the National Publishers' Association.

HIBBARD. Oh, yes, yes, I remember. Please—sit right down, Mr. Ganning. (*Bringing a chair into place at the desk.*) Mrs.—ah—Creeley— (*Indicates a chair at the table* R.)

MRS. CREEVEY. Creevey. Louella May Creevey.

HIBBARD. Oh, yes.

MRS. CREEVEY. Justice Hibbard, before we go any further, I *must* tell you how much we admire your record on the bench. Ever since your vote in the Rosika Schwimmer case you have consistently upheld our contention that women are not women—they are persons! Because we do not want to be discriminated *for* any more than *against*—we will not tolerate laws that discriminate between the sexes *as* sexes. In a larger sense, there *is* no sex. *Is* there, Mrs. Hibbard?

IRENE. (*Stumped.*) Well—in a larger sense.

MRS. CREEVEY. (*Crossing to the table* R.) I knew you would agree with me. (*She starts to sit.*) I hope I'm not taking your chair? (*Sits* L. *of table.*)

IRENE. No, no. That's quite all right.

(GANNING *sits* L. *of desk.* HIBBARD *sits* R. *of desk.*)

MRS. CREEVEY. (*Settling herself.*) Ah, what a beautiful room! So warm, so human! And books, books! Books make a room so livable. I'm sure you and the Justice must spend many happy hours here, Mrs. Hibbard.

IRENE. Oh, many.

MASON. I always liked this room. And that desk of yours, Carter—same one he had in Cleveland, on the Appellate bench.

MRS. CREEVEY. Ah, what a wonderful thing it is—to preserve one's simplicity!

GANNING. That's very true. When I was a poor country boy, breaking the ice in the water pitcher before I could wash, I resolved that I would never lose the common touch, no matter how successful I became. And although today the Ganning newspapers have a combined morning and evening circulation of twenty million copies, I hope I can truthfully say that I am still that country boy at heart.

IRENE. (*Starting to cross* U.R.) Well, if you'll excuse me— I'm sure I'd only be in your way.

MRS. CREEVEY. Oh, no, Mrs. Hibbard! Just the contrary!

MASON. We need *you* too, Irene.

GANNING. You are a vital part of this, Mrs. Hibbard, I assure you.

IRENE. (*Coming down.*) (*Puzzled.*) Really?

MASON. Yes, indeed. . . . Well, people, what do you say? Shall we get under way?

GANNING. All right.

MRS. CREEVEY. I'm ready!

MASON. (*Clearing his throat and trying to put the whole thing on an informal basis.*) Carter, we feel that these are pretty ticklish times. When Mrs. Creevey came to me—as a boyhood friend of yours—with the suggestion that I am about to present to you, my first reaction was: George Mason, why didn't *you* think of that long ago? Then I said to myself, now, who is the man that can get behind this thing and put it over? Well, sir, there was only one answer —Ellsworth T. Ganning, of the Ganning newspapers. (*Pats* GANNING *on shoulder.*) Carter, we feel that what the country needs—and when I say "we" I am speaking for the Bar Association—we feel that with all the changes made in the Constitution latterly, it wouldn't be a bad idea to have a President who understood administering it, let alone had read it. And I speak for the State Association, too.

HIBBARD. President? You mean—of the Bar Association?

MRS. CREEVEY. Ah, what modesty!

MASON. No, Carter. I mean the Presidency of the United States.

HIBBARD. (*Rises—*GANNING *also rises.*) Why— Why—

MASON. Now don't say a word yet. Not a word. We want you to think seriously before answering.

MRS. CREEVEY. (*Rises.*) And you too, Mrs. Hibbard. I know what your first thought is—it is of *him.* The strain, the burden of it all. Can he bear it?

MASON. Say! Anybody that can wade all day in a trout stream—eh, Carter?

HIBBARD. (*Crossing to* MASON.) (*Still in a daze.*) Oh, yes, yes. . . . Well, may I say that this is—pretty overwhelming.

MASON. I don't blame you. It overwhelmed me at first.

HIBBARD. But—does this mean I would have to resign from the Supreme bench?

MASON. Oh, not for a long while. Nobody's to know about this for weeks—we're not breathing a word.

MRS. CREEVEY. Not even a syllable! Millions of women are keeping perfectly quiet.

MASON. All we want *now* is permission to sound people out —very quietly.

GANNING. Then, when the time comes, we shoot! Announcement, publicity—why, I'll put your pictures on the front page of twenty million newspapers every day, right opposite my signed editorial. You can't lose, Mr. Justice. *Now!* What do you say?

MASON. It's up to *you,* Carter.

MRS. CREEVEY. The women of America are hanging on your words.

MASON. Well?

HIBBARD. Gentlemen—and Mrs. Creevey. (*A step to her.*) I am of course engrossed in the honorable position I occupy. I regard with repugnance the strifes and partisanships of political life. Also, in the last analysis, there is a personal element involved. (*Keeping his eyes on* IRENE.) Any decision of this magnitude must rest with—my dear wife.

MRS. CREEVEY. How sweet! How too, too sweet!

GANNING. (*With a flourish.*) Well, Mrs. Hibbard?

MASON. First Lady of the Land, Irene!

(WARN CURTAIN.)

MRS. CREEVEY. America waits!

IRENE. (*Crossing to* HIBBARD.) What can I say? My husband's interests are mine; his life is mine. I can but follow him, even though it means giving up the peace and quiet of our own fireside. (*Kisses him.*)

MRS. CREEVEY. Oh! Beautiful!

GANNING. Great! Then we can go right to work.

MASON. And we're going to put you over, too!

GANNING. (*Crossing to* IRENE.) You know the first picture I'm going to print? You and Mrs. Hibbard sitting in this room, just the way I found you here tonight. Just the way millions of American couples sit home every night, talking over the day's work, listening to the radio.

IRENE. Oh, yes, he does both. Don't you, Carter? We hurry through dinner every night, so that he can hear the Whoops Family.

MRS. CREEVEY. How human!

IRENE. And of course he reads detective stories. (*She picks up* "Murder in the Phone Booth!") They relax him.

GANNING. Like Woodrow Wilson!

MRS. CREEVEY. Ah, it's so wonderful to relax! I often say to Mr. Creevey—he is one of the largest manufacturers of bed-ticking in the country, and is more tense than most people realize—I often say to him: If you only would relax, Irving—

IRENE. Oh, Carter's wonderful that way. I have no trouble with him at all.

GANNING. And Mason tells me you're a fisherman, too. That's all good rotogravure, you know. Hip boots, basket, that sort of thing.

IRENE. Oh, yes, indeed. Like Calvin Coolidge.

MRS. CREEVEY. (*Worshipfully.*) Calvin Coolidge!

IRENE. (*Indicating the atrocity on the wall.*) That's an American amberjack. Caught off the Coast of Florida, February twenty-sixth, nineteen hundred and seventeen.

MRS. CREEVEY. Think of it! She knows the very date!

GANNING. A real American wife, that's what she is! You know what I want from you, Mrs. Hibbard? A daily feature article on home-making. How to put up quince preserves, make your own dresses, apple pie, all the good old American dishes!

IRENE. I'd be delighted.

MRS. CREEVEY. She'll be another Dolly Madison!

GANNING. Wonderful, wonderful!

IRENE. But of course I only know the simplest dishes— (*She seats* HIBBARD *in chair at the table*) because Carter has such a delicate stomach.

GANNING. A delicate stomach! That's marvelous! That'll appeal to people all over the country! Don't you think so, Mason?

MASON. I certainly do.

GANNING. You bet it will. Do you know how many people in this country have got bad stomachs? Millions! Millions!

MRS. CREEVEY. (*Beaming.*) Mr. Creevey has one!

IRENE. Darling, you mustn't forget your tablets. (*Crosses to the desk for tablets. Shakes out tablets.*)

MRS. CREEVEY. Ah!

(CURTAIN STARTS DOWN.)

IRENE. (*She is cramming soda tablets down the judicial throat as she speaks.*) You know, if I don't look after him he just doesn't do a thing for himself . . . just a great big baby, really . . .

(*Simultaneously, on* IRENE'S *business with tablets.*)

MRS. CREEVEY. A wonderful wife, that's what she is!

GANNING. A pictorial campaign — that's what we're going to have! We'll have a staff photographer here tomorrow afternoon!

MASON. That's right! That's what they'll understand. Pictures —Pictures!

MEDIUM FAST CURTAIN

ACT II

Scene II

(WARN CLOCK STRIKE.)

The Wayne living room.

(LIGHTS.)

Rather late in the evening—the room empty and dimly lit. After a moment the dining-room doors are opened, by STEPHEN WAYNE—*there is a burst of masculine laughter as he does so. One gets a glimpse of three or four men around the dining-room table—white shirt front, heavy cigar smoke, crumpled napkins, demi-tasses.*

As curtain rises a clock strikes on the mantel. Eleven—

(CLOCK STRIKES ELEVEN.)

STEPHEN. (*As he emerges.*) I tell you they've a horse named after you! And I'll prove it to you!

(*He comes into the room and gathers up the evening paper. Meanwhile the crowd in the dining room is in a heavily jocular mood—there is another burst of laughter, followed by* HARDWICK'S *voice which rises above the noise:* "Which end of the horse was it, Stephen?" *Another laugh.*)

STEPHEN. (*Returning with the paper.*) Here you are! He ran down in Florida today. His name is Tightwad!

(*A much bigger laugh this time, as* STEPHEN *closes the doors.*)

(LUCY *and* GORDON KEANE *enter from the hall* U.R. LUCY *is*

69

in evening clothes and wrap; KEANE *in tails and high hat.*)

LUCY. Oh, of course you can. They're still in there talking—they'll be there for hours. ~~Turn on the lights, will you?~~ ~~Right there, beside the door.~~ (*He switches on the lights.*)
(BRACKET LIGHTS.)
~~That's right.~~ . . . Well, I must say that you set up a very nice evening, Senator. (*She turns on table lamps.*) Flowers,
(TABLE LIGHTS.)
dinner, theatre—what more could a girl ask? (*Turns on desk lamp.*)

(DESK LIGHT.)

KEANE. (*Taking off his coat; putting it on chair* L. *of table* D.R.) I'm sorry the play wasn't better. I thought it would be something worth seeing. A year in New York.

LUCY. Yes, but that doesn't mean much any more—a year in New York. With traffic the way it is over there, it takes them six months just to get to the theatre.

CHARLES. (*Entering.*) Do you wish anything, Madam?

LUCY. Senator, will you have a drink?

KEANE. No, thank you.

LUCY. No, thank you, Charles! What are they doing in there, Charles? Just dawdling over the coffee and burning holes in the tablecloth?

CHARLES. Yes, ma'am, but I gave them one of the old ones, so there's no harm done. (*He exits* U.L.)

(KEANE *crosses down below table* R.)

LUCY. Why *do* men love to sit over a dinner table with wadded up napkins and melted ice cream? (*She is at her desk, looking through her mail.*) Do sit down, Senator. (*She looks at the things in her hand, crossing to* C.) Bills. Bills. Hotel Shoreham. Cocktail Hour—4:30 to 7. You know it's calling that an hour that has put this country where it is today.

KEANE. (*A step in to* LUCY.) Look! I—I'd like awfully to tell you about my agricultural bill. Do you mind?

LUCY. No, not at all. I'd love to hear about it. But just very simply. Words of one syllable.

KEANE. All right. Now, take that telephone receiver.

LUCY. Oh, that's fine. I can understand that. A telephone receiver.

KEANE. Well, in our State Experimental Laboratories, they've worked out a way to make that very same thing out of ordinary cornstalks.

LUCY. Cornstalks? You don't tell me?

KEANE. You see what it means, don't you? To the farmer?

LUCY. Of course. He can call up from any place in the cornfield. . . . Oh, here's Emmy.

(*The voice of* EMMY *is heard in the hall:* "Oh, sure she is. I hear her talking.")

(EMMY *enters—bubbling over with vitality, and squired by a good-looking young man named* JASON FLEMING. *Both are in evening clothes. He is carrying overcoat, muffler, top hat;* EMMY'S *handbag is in his coat pocket.*)

JASON. Good evening, Mrs. Wayne.

LUCY. Oh, here's Emmy!

EMMY. Oh, Aunt Lucy, we had the most marvelous time!

LUCY. Senator Keane, my—

EMMY. Senator, mighty nice to see you.

KEANE. Good evening, Miss Paige.

LUCY. Gordon, this is Jason Fleming. Senator Keane, Jason.

(*The* MEN *exchange greetings.*)

EMMY. I declare I never did see anything so beautiful as that Italian Embassy, and the Ambassador was the cutest thing. I like to died he was so cute. Everybody there was a signora or an excellency or something—I just couldn't take my eyes off that Countess Di What's-Her-Name—you know, that stunning one that sort of unwinds when she gets up.

LUCY. Well, it all seems to have been a great success, Emmy. Who took you in?

EMMY. (*In fresh raptures.*) The most beautiful attaché in the Embassy—or in the whole world, I reckon. Where's the card, Jason? The one the gentlemen get downstairs to find the ladies by?

JASON. (*Producing her evening bag.*) I told her to relax, Mrs. Wayne—that Mussolini makes them resign from the Diplomatic Service if they marry out of their country.

KEANE. That's one law of his I approve of.

EMMY. You-all are just mean. (*She finds the card.*) Here it is—I made him give it to me for my scrapbook. Conte Guilio—(*She pronounces it "Julio."*)

LUCY. Jee-lio, Emmy.

EMMY. Yes, that's what he said. Conte Jeelie Giordano. Isn't that darling? I got his autograph, too. (*She exhibits it.*)

LUCY. That ought to be worth something.

EMMY. And here's a picture of the whole table. Entree— that's where you go in, see—isn't it cute having it in French? I was just dying to ask Jee-ulio all about everything but all through supper they kept playing music—you couldn't talk at all.

LUCY. (*Puts bills on desk.*) That's why they have the music, Emmy. That's called diplomacy.

(EMMY *puts wrap on* U.L. *table.*)

JASON. I hope you never write a book about us, Mrs. Wayne. You know too many of the tricks.

LUCY. You're the one to do that, Jason. (EMMY *sits on arm of chair* U.L.) (*To* KEANE.) You know, if it weren't for this man we'd be at war all the time. (*A step to* C.) How's the latest imbroglio, Jason?

JASON. Well, we're still working on it.

LUCY. (*To* KEANE *again.*) Somebody slipped up on the entrance cards for the White House diplomatic reception, and one of them—which country was it, Jason?—got delivered at the wrong door with the ice-cream or something.

JASON. Oh, that was Germany. And the worst of it was it was French ice-cream.

LUCY. You see the complications.

KEANE. (*A little laugh.*) Yes, indeed.

LUCY. Tell me, Jason—how's the Near East? Is Trans-Bulgania still speaking to us?

JASON. Well, it looks as though they're coming around.

LUCY. You know, Jason knows more about the Balkans than they do themselves. All these little new countries that spring up after every rain—he knows them all.

KEANE. Well, I think I'd better be going. It must be getting pretty late.

JASON. Me too. I've got to be diplomatic at nine a.m. sharp.

KEANE. (*After an appropriate laugh.*) Well, good night, Mrs. Wayne.

LUCY. Good night, Senator. And thank you.

KEANE. Now look, there's a hearing on the bill at nine o'clock tomorrow morning. You'll be there, won't you?

LUCY. Nine o'clock? I'll tell you what—suppose I send Emmy in my place? She's never seen a hearing.

EMMY. (*Coming down stage.*) What?

LUCY. Wouldn't you like that, Emmy? Up at the Capitol? Because I just remembered I have another engagement.

EMMY. Oh, I'd love to! Can I ride in the elevator with you? (*She turns to* JASON.) You know, when you're a Senator you ring the elevator bell three times, and the elevator man comes and gets you right away, no matter who's on it, and takes you wherever you want to go, without stopping for anybody.

LUCY. Well, this is a democracy.

EMMY. Oh, I just thought of something! Why don't I begin collecting Senators?

LUCY. What?

EMMY. Autographs, I mean.

LUCY. Oh! You scared the life out of me, Emmy.

KEANE. I don't think you'd have a bit of trouble, Miss Paige. Well—good night. (JASON *crosses* U.C.)

EMMY. (*Takes* KEANE's *arm.*) I'll take you out to the door.

KEANE. Oh, thanks.

JASON. Good night, Mrs. Wayne.

LUCY. Good night, Jason.

EMMY. What time do you want me to be there?

KEANE. Well, the hearing starts at nine o'clock.

EMMY. I'll get there at half-past eight. (*Exits* U.R.)

(LUCY *puts her coat on chair* R. *of table and rings the bell* U.R. *for the* BUTLER.)

(*As the trio disappears* SOPHY *comes in* D.L. *from the drawing room. Black afternoon dress; hat on; carrying her coat. She brings with her a* brief case *and a* stack of addressed envelopes *which she puts on the desk.*)

SOPHY. Oh, I didn't know you were back.

LUCY. Sophy, darling! At this ghastly hour! Didn't you go home?

SOPHY. Well, it seemed a heaven-sent opportunity to do the invitations for your Diplomatic Corps dinner. It's the trickiest job—I only trust myself with it.

(CHARLES *starts on.*)

LUCY. You must be dead. Don't you want a drink or something?

SOPHY. (*Sits at desk.*) No, thanks. . . . Did you have a pleasant evening? How was the play?

LUCY. Oh, fair. (*As* CHARLES *enters* U.C.) Charles, do something about getting the men out of there, will you? Nothing drastic, you understand—just something subtle, like pulling Senator Hardwick's chair from under him, or yelling "Fire!" or something.

CHARLES. I'll try, madam. (*He starts to go.*)

LUCY. You didn't forget to serve his coffee in a big cup, did you, Charles? With cream.

CHARLES. (*As he goes* U.L.) No, ma'am. I remembered.

SOPHY. Well, tell me all about it. How are you and the Boy Senator getting along?

LUCY. (*Taking a long breath.*) Oh, *very* well. *Too* well. Sophy, he has a plan—you must get him to tell you about it —he's going to make typewriter ribbons out of skim milk or something, and save the American farmer. Of course I've been making silk purses out of sows' ears all my life, but I didn't tell him that.

SOPHY. You seem to be picking up where Irene left off.

LUCY. (*Brightening immediately.*) Sophy, she was at the theatre. Sitting in a box with her Presidential timber. They were so beautifully connubial. She actually believes it, Sophy. Isn't that wonderful? It was a *great* success, Sophy, the whole idea. And it was worth doing, in spite of Gordon.

SOPHY. Speaking of Gordon, what are you going to do with him now that you've got him?

LUCY. (*Crossing over* R.) Well, I had a little inspiration there. At least, I think I did. Emmy. She'll just love these typewriter ribbons.

SOPHY. Why don't you open a day nursery?

(*Enter* TOM HARDWICK. *Comes through the dining-room doors. We hear his voice as the door opens:* "Well, you fellows don't know anything.—I'm going to talk to a real politician." *Then* STEPHEN'S VOICE *is heard:* "Who's out there? Lucy? You'd better look out for her!")

HARDWICK. (SOPHY *rises—Exits* D.L.) Gosh, what a dinner you gave us, Lucy! Not a company dish in the lot! That's the way vegetable soup ought to be made. Good and thick —you ought to be able to skate on soup stock.

LUCY. Tell me—it's been a pretty long huddle in there. What's it all about?

HARDWICK. (*Crosses to* L.) I wish to God I knew—I never heard so much tripe in my life. Who does this Ganning think he is, anyhow?

LUCY. Ssh! Don't ask him—he'll tell you.

HARDWICK. All right, he's in the newspaper business, but when they've got a good business of their own why do they think they have to mix into politics? What's politics got to do with business? What's back of it, anyhow? Has he got a wife that wants to be an Ambassador or something? (*Crosses back to* LUCY.)

LUCY. Well, it's nice work if you can get it. (*Crossing to* R.)

HARDWICK. Now, Sedgwick—he's different. I don't mind bankers. As long as they keep their mouth shut and pay the bills. . . . But Ganning! Why, he's Public Opinion himself.

GANNING. (*Emerging from the conclave* U.C.) Well, we didn't know what we were missing! Good evening, Mrs. Wayne.

LUCY. Mr. Ganning.

GANNING. Mrs. Wayne, Mrs. Ganning told me I mustn't come home without your promise to dine with us next time you're in New York. Now what are you going to do about it?

LUCY. Well, I wouldn't stand in the way of your going home for anything.

GANNING. That's fine. Mrs. Ganning'll be delighted. (*He finds himself next to* TOM HARDWICK.) Got a match, Hardwick? (*Feeling for a match.*)

HARDWICK. (*Who wouldn't give him one if he had.*) No!

(*The last two diners,* STEPHEN WAYNE *and* HERBERT SEDG-
WICK, *have come out of the dining room.* EMMY *returns at
the same time from* U.R. *The men leave the dining-room
doors open.*)

EMMY. Hello, Uncle Stephen!

STEPHEN. Emmy—Well, we're finally out of the dining room,
anyhow. Had you given us up, Lucy?

LUCY. Hello, darling. Mr. Sedgwick, how are *you?*

SEDGWICK. A little groggy, after that session. I guess I'm
spoiled by directors' meetings.

STEPHEN. Yes, you business men just get together, vote
yourselves a bonus, and in five minutes it's all over.

SEDGWICK. Ganning, oughtn't we to be on our way? (*Turns
to the others.*) We've got to catch a train to New York.

GANNING. Okay! Well—seems to me we're all set. (*Crossing
to* STEPHEN.) Mr. Secretary, you represent the President
more or less. You say he won't put up any hurdles.

STEPHEN. Well, of course that has to be handled delicately.
An outgoing President must not seem to be dictating his
successor—

HARDWICK. (*In a low voice.*) Although it's been done.

STEPHEN. And at the same time it's bad for the party if he
doesn't approve. You've got to catch it just *so.*

(HARDWICK *crosses* U.L.)

LUCY. (*Who has been drinking this in.*) What is all this?
Don't tell me you've picked a candidate! And kept it from
me all this time!

STEPHEN. Well, it isn't *set* yet, Lucy—

LUCY. (*In high excitement.*) Who is it? *You've* got it set! Who is it?

GANNING. Well, you understand that this is off the record, Mrs. Wayne—

(*Enter* SOPHY, D.L.)

HARDWICK. (*Crosses D. stage.*) *She* knows that! She's heard more off the record than you've put *on!* It's Carter Hibbard!

LUCY. (*In the voice of a stricken woman.*) What? (*There is a pause as* STEPHEN *crosses to back of the table.*)

HARDWICK. (*Bitterly.*) It seems we need a man who can interpret the laws of the country, and we got so God-damned many now that it takes a Supreme Court Justice to do it. (*Crosses U.L.*)

LUCY. (*Recovering herself—Sits L. of table.*) But—Carter Hibbard! How—how did you ever come to select *him?*

HARDWICK. Well, if you ask me I don't see yet how it happened.

GANNING. He's the logical candidate, that's all.

HARDWICK. Well, maybe. I'm not crazy about him, but there's no denying he's got the jump on us.

LUCY. (*Looking up at* STEPHEN.) Stephen!

STEPHEN. There just seems to be a lot of Hibbard sentiment, Lucy. We don't know how it started—

GANNING. Spontaneously, I assure you.

STEPHEN. Anyhow, it certainly exists, and it's sort of taken us by surprise. The women's clubs are back of him solid, and the bar associations. Taking the whole thing together, it looks as though he's got a head start.

GANNING. Well, I don't see where you'd get a better man. (*Crossing* D.L.) A poor boy, born in Kentucky—there's a doubtful State to begin with, Kentucky. (*Crossing to* C.) Studied law in Ohio—there's the Lincoln touch. Country home in Virginia—another doubtful State. Fishes every year in Wisconsin and Florida—I tell you, he's a natural.

HARDWICK. Well, I hope ~~to God~~ you're right.

LUCY. But—he isn't known to the country. It takes years to build up a Presidential candidate. . . .

SEDGWICK. Not today it doesn't. Thanks to the radio.

GANNING. And the Ganning newspapers.

SEDGWICK. Yes, of course.

LUCY. But—have you been to him? Has he accepted already?

GANNING. Oh, I think we can wangle that.

HARDWICK. (*Morbidly.*) I'm afraid so.

GANNING. As a matter of fact, he's written a most human document on that very point. If you gentlemen will bear with me, I'd like to read it to Mrs. Wayne.

LUCY. I'd be delighted.

GANNING. At the proper moment I shall publish this in the Ganning papers.

LUCY. I'm sure.

(EMMY *sits* R. *of table.*)

GANNING. (*Reads.*) "My dear Ellsworth: Replying to your courteous note, I can only say that your inquiry regarding my candidacy is only one of many that have come to me, and therefore I cannot longer postpone expressing my feelings on the subject. I am not a candidate for the nomination."

EMMY. He isn't going to *take* it?

LUCY. Emmy!

GANNING. "My present duty and responsibilities should satisfy any man who desires to render public service. They satisfy me, and I have no inclination to relinquish them. But—"

LUCY. I see.

EMMY. Maybe he's going to change his mind.

GANNING. "But my wishes may not coincide with my duty. If it be true, as many responsible people assure me, that a decided majority of the better element—"

HARDWICK. Better element!

GANNING. "Are insistent that I accept the nomination for this great office, I shall deem it my duty, as well as an honor and a privilege, to do so. With every assurance of my best wishes, my dear Ellsworth, I am yours most sincerely, Carter Hibbard."

LUCY. Well, that sounds definite, doesn't it?

SEDGWICK. Personally, I feel that he can be persuaded.

STEPHEN. You know, hearing that letter for the second time, it kind of grows on you, doesn't it?

GANNING. Yes, it does, doesn't it?

SEDGWICK. Well, Ganning, we'd better get to the train. Sorry to run, Mrs. Wayne, but you understand. (*Starts up.*)

GANNING. Mrs. Wayne, my thanks for a delightful evening. And a most fruitful one. I feel that history has been made in this house tonight.

LUCY. Hasn't it, though?

SEDGWICK. Good night!

GANNING. Good night, everyone. Good night, Hardwick.

HARDWICK. Good night!

SEDGWICK. (*Making his adieus to his host.*) Mr. Secretary.

STEPHEN. (*Moving with them to the door.*) Sorry you have to go. (*He turns to* HARDWICK.) Tom, you're not catching any trains. Why don't you wait a minute?

HARDWICK. Okay! (*With a few more good-byes* STEPHEN *takes* SEDGWICK *and* GANNING *out* U.R.)

EMMY. (*Rises.*) Isn't it exciting? Is this the way they make Presidents—just sort of at home like this?

LUCY. It's fantastic, Tom! It's incredible!

HARDWICK. Yes, but it looks as though we're in for it. Funny thing about it, Lucy, I wouldn't be surprised if we won with him. Supreme Court, and he sort of looks like a President. *They* don't know he's full of sawdust.

LUCY. No. I suppose not.

EMMY. (*A sudden pause.*) I just thought of something. Does this mean Mrs. Hibbard is going to be the First Lady? And be in the White House and everything?

LUCY. (*After a pause.*) Emmy, why don't you run up to bed?

EMMY. (*Starts up.*) (*Reluctant.*) Well—all right. You're sure nothing else is going to happen?

LUCY. No. Everything has happened, Emmy.

EMMY. (*Taking her coat.*) Well, if you're sure. Good night, then. (*She exits* U.L. *and* SOPHY *exits* D.L.)

HARDWICK. Good night. Sorry, Lucy. I never thought of that Irene angle. Well, you girls'll just have to kiss and make up, I guess. . . . Golly, I hate to face Belle!

LUCY. I hate to face myself.

HARDWICK. You know, Lucy, I wasn't going to say anything till it came off, but—we sort of had our hearts set on swinging this for Stephen.

LUCY. Oh, don't, Tom.

HARDWICK. Hadn't been for this Hibbard business we could have done it, too. Even had the President with us. Then Ganning crashed through with all these clubwomen behind him—God, I wish women would keep out of politics.

LUCY. (*Ever so quietly.*) Mm—So do I.

HARDWICK. Well—too bad. Would have been kind of right— Stephen in the White House. (LUCY *rises—crosses to* R. *Puts coat on chair* R.) And *you* there again, Lucy—it would have been kind of right. (*He looks at the portrait.*) Andy would have liked it, too.

(STEPHEN *saunters back from the hallway* U.R.)

STEPHEN. Want to thresh a while, Tom?

HARDWICK. (*As he starts out* U.C.) What the hell is there to thresh about? We're in for it and we might as well go ahead. (*Crosses* D.U.L. *Exits.*)

STEPHEN. Yes, I guess you're right. How about you, Lucy? Want to come along?

LUCY. No. Thank you, Stephen. (STEPHEN *starts* U.C.) Stephen?

STEPHEN. Yes, dear. (*He comes toward her.*)

(HARDWICK *is gone. There is a moment's pause as* LUCY *tries to decide how to begin.*)

LUCY. Stephen, you know I love you, don't you?

STEPHEN. Well, I hope so.   (WARN CURTAIN.)

LUCY. No, I mean it. I do love you, Stephen. I do love you.

STEPHEN. (*Surprised at the depth of her tone.*) Why, Lucy!

LUCY. I just wanted to say it, that's all. I love you.

STEPHEN. Now Lucy, it's all right. You mustn't feel badly about *me*. I won't say I wouldn't have liked it—at least I'd be sure then that the work of these last years wouldn't be tipped over. But—you've just got to put it out of your mind. It's all right.

LUCY. I wish I could take it like you, Stephen. But I can't— I can't! It kills me.

STEPHEN. We've got to be sports about it—that's all there is to it. . . . Funny it has to be Irene, isn't it?

LUCY. Yes, isn't it?

STEPHEN. I'm so sorry, my dear. I'm so sorry to have failed you.

LUCY. (*Holding back the tears.*) Stephen, my darling! Don't! Don't!

STEPHEN. Come now—this isn't like you.

LUCY. Oh, Stephen! Stephen! Stephen!

STEPHEN. (*Comforting her.*) I know. I know.

LUCY. (*Slowly coming out of it.*) I'm all right now.

STEPHEN. Of course you are. . . . I ought to run along, dear. Sure you're all right? (*She smiles at him.*) Coming up?

LUCY. In a minute. Finish up with Tom.

(*He kisses her—tenderly, affectionately. A little smile passes between them when it's all over. He goes. For an appreciable interval* LUCY *stands there, motionless. She looks at the portrait. Then* SOPHY *enters—quietly, knowing the whole situation, eager to pretend that nothing has happened.* LUCY *barely notices her as she moves about her work.*)

SOPHY. (*Gathering up a few envelopes from the desk: speaking entirely too casually.*) These have to be delivered by hand in the morning.

LUCY. How could I, Sophy? How could I have done it? Poor Stephen! That's what I can't forgive myself—what I've done to Stephen!

SOPHY. Well, you might have known something like this would happen. You just got caught, that's all.

LUCY. How was I to know? Do you think for a minute I would have deliberately jeopardized Stephen's chances if I'd known? Who'd ever *believe* they'd do a thing like this? Carter Hibbard! Oh, if only I'd never met that woman!

SOPHY. What woman?

LUCY. You know, with the affiliated bodies. If only I'd never met her!

SOPHY. Anyhow, it's done. But this ought to be a lesson to you.

LUCY. (L. *of the table.*) Yes . . . Yes. . . . I've got nothing to say for myself, Sophy. Nothing at all. But to think of *me* turning out to be one of those meddling Washington women—the kind of women I've always despised, Sophy—and then I go and do the same thing myself! To think of *me* being responsible for putting Carter Hibbard in the White House! I won't have it, Sophy—that's all. I won't have it!

SOPHY. Well, it looks as though you're *going* to have it.

LUCY. (*Crossing to* SOPHY.) Well, I won't! And Irene, Sophy! Irene as First Lady—I won't have it! I tell you I won't have her in those rooms!

SOPHY. Now, Lucy—

LUCY. (*Crossing to* C.) I won't, I won't! I'd use anything. Do you think *he'd* have stood by and let a thing like this happen? No! Because first and last he was a politician! Do you know what he did once? He locked his delegates in a hotel room and walked around with the key in his pocket! For two days! And do you know what Abraham Lincoln did? He jumped out of a window so he wouldn't have to have his vote recorded! Because *he* was a politician, too! And so *am* I! Grandpa, Lincoln and *me,* Sophy! And if we can't beat Irene Hibbard with a ticket like that, there's something wrong with Lincoln and Grandpa! (*Curtain starts down.*) Now, I'll tell you what we're going to do! The first thing tomorrow morning—

FAST CURTAIN

ACT III

SCENE: *The scene is again the Secretary of State's home—some time in the afternoon of an early Spring day. Sitting there as the curtain rises is* EMMY—EMMY *in trig riding clothes, and looking very attractive indeed. She is reading, sitting* L. *of the table* D.R.

CHARLES *passes through the hall. Crosses* R. *to* L. *Carrying vase.*

EMMY. Oh, Charles!

CHARLES. Yes, miss?

EMMY. (*Indicating a sizable pile of magazines at her elbow.*) Is this all there are of the Congressional Records?

CHARLES. There may be some more in Mrs. Wayne's room. Shall I get them?

EMMY. Well—not now. These'll last me a little while.

(*She settles herself, with a good deal of squirming, and takes another Record as* CHARLES *goes out. She opens it with high hopes, but the first page turns out to be rather dull. She pokes into it a little further, but there are still no pictures. She puts it down and tries another.* SOPHY *comes in* U.R.—*from the other hallway, and with hat and coat on. She carries a few small packages, and is her usual business-like self.*)

SOPHY. (*Coming down* C.) Oh, hello there! Been riding?

EMMY. No, not yet. I'm just waiting to go.

87

SOPHY. (*Mildly surprised.*) What are you reading? The Congressional Record?

(*Enter* CHARLES U.L.)

EMMY. Uh-huh.

SOPHY. And all those too?

EMMY. Well, I haven't read 'em *yet,* but I'm going to.

SOPHY. You've got a busy summer. (CHARLES *has meanwhile entered. He takes* SOPHY'S *coat.*) Any messages, Charles? Did the cards come from the printer?

CHARLES. Yes, Miss. They're right on the desk.

SOPHY. Oh, fine. Let's see— (*Crosses below* CHARLES *to desk* L.) the flowers won't be here till six. What did they say about the terrapin? Was it all right?

CHARLES. Yes, Miss Prescott.

SOPHY. I'll see you later about the table. I think we'll use the lace cloth and the silver epergnes. *Candlesticks*

CHARLES. Yes, Miss. (*He goes* U.L.)

SOPHY. (*Sits.*) Well, I might as well get at it. (*She takes up the packet of cards.*)

EMMY. (*Rises—crosses to* SOPHY.) Oh, that's cute. Is that tonight's dinner?

SOPHY. Now, don't touch anything, Emmy. (*She picks up a handful of place-markers.*)

EMMY. Oh, what are you going to do with those?

SOPHY. They mark where people sit, Emmy. The green ones are men and the white ones are women. (*She puts a couple of markers into their slots.*) See?

EMMY. They look just like little tombstones. (*A look from* SOPHY.) Am I at the dinner?

SOPHY. I don't know yet. You may have to fill in.

EMMY. (*Crossing back to table.*) Is Gordon going to be there?

SOPHY. Yes, he is.

EMMY. Oh! (*She strolls back to her chair, thoughtfully.*)

SOPHY. (*Busily writing.*) So it's Gordon now, is it?

EMMY. What?

SOPHY. You're calling him Gordon now.

EMMY. My goodness, you can't keep calling him Senator. (*Sits L. of table.*)

SOPHY. No, I suppose not. (*There is a pause as she works away.*) Oh, dear! Where can you seat an ex-American Ambassador? They don't belong anywhere, and they're so touchy.

EMMY. (*Who has been absorbed in her Records again.*) What did you say?

SOPHY. Hostess troubles, Emmy. I was just talking to myself. (*They settle to their respective tasks.*)

EMMY. What's the St. Lawrence water-wave?

SOPHY. The what?

EMMY. The St. Lawrence water-wave?

SOPHY. Not a wave, Emmy. Way. Waterway.

EMMY. (*Looks again.*) Oh, yes. I thought it sounded funny. . . . (*Reading*) "I move to strike out in line 24 the word 'and' and insert the word 'but.'" My goodness, wouldn't you think they'd have something better to do, with things the way they are?

SOPHY. Yes, you really would, Emmy.

EMMY. And what's it mean when they order a resolution to lie on the table? They never did that while I was up there.

SOPHY. That just means they want it out of the way, Emmy.

EMMY. Well, wouldn't it be even more in the way on the table?

SOPHY. They don't mean a real table, Emmy.

EMMY. Then why do they say table?

SOPHY. It's just an expression.

EMMY. Well, here it says Senator Cartwright took the chair. Is it a real chair?

SOPHY. Yes, it *is* a real chair.   (WARN DOOR BELL.)

EMMY. (*Rises—crosses to* C.) Well, why do they have a real chair and not a real table?

SOPHY. (*At her wits' end.*) Oh! . . . Why don't you ask Senator Keane about it? Let him explain it.

EMMY. That's just it. I don't want him to know that I don't know.

SOPHY. I'm sure he'll never guess.

EMMY. (*Back to table.*) I wish I knew as much as Aunt Lucy does.

SOPHY. (*With meaning.*) Maybe it's just as well you don't.

EMMY. (*Going into a semi-trance.*) Let's see: Monday, Justices of the Supreme Court; Tuesday, Congressmen; Wednesday, the Cabinet; Thursday, Senators; and Friday, Diplomatic.

SOPHY. (*Who has only half heard all this.*) What are you muttering about, anyhow?

EMMY. I was just seeing if I remembered the different At-Home days. Monday, Justices of the Supreme Court—

(DOOR BELL.)

(*The door bell rings.*) Oh, I reckon this is him. (*Puts pile of Congressional Records on the couch.*)

SOPHY. Who's coming? Gordon?

(CHARLES *crosses* L. *to* R.)

EMMY. Hm. You'd think that old Senate would be ashamed of itself, keeping 'em all in on a day like this. Here it is pretty near four o'clock.

SOPHY. Oh, it's a dog's life. Some days they can only play about eighteen holes.

EMMY. Well, Gordon works awful hard. Last night, at the movies, he was writing a speech all during Jean Harlow. *Joan Crawf*

SOPHY. Sounds like the perfect place to me.

(SENATOR KEANE *enters* U.R. *Also in riding clothes.*)

KEANE. They told me to come right in.

EMMY. (*Getting into her coat which is on chair back of table.*) I'm all ready. See how prompt I am?

KEANE. How do you do, Miss Prescott?

SOPHY. Senator.

EMMY. I thought they weren't ever going to let you go. I was going to come right up there and get you.

KEANE. (*Crosses to* SOPHY.) I wouldn't have minded that. (*As* EMMY *adjusts her hat.*) Miss Prescott, too bad you have to stay and work on a day like this.

SOPHY. Oh, this isn't work. I'm just playing paper dolls.

EMMY. (*Crosses to* SOPHY.) Sophy's fixing the places for tonight's dinner. Oh, where's Gordon going to sit? Show Gordon where he's going to sit.

SOPHY. Well, I'm not sure yet.

EMMY. Yes, you are! (*She leans over and reads the cards.*) You've got Mrs. Archibald Wellington on one side—she's the Vice-President's daughter—and Madame von Langendonch— (*She has a good deal of trouble with this one*) —on the other. Who's she?

SOPHY. She's the wife of the Dutch chargé d'affaires.

EMMY. Oh, yes, I know her. Oh, (*Crosses to* R.C.) they're both terribly brainy—they know all about everything. After you talk to them you won't ever want to see poor little me again.

KEANE. (*Follows her.*) Now, you know better than that.

EMMY. Oh, but I mean it. Because I'm not bright the way they are—there's nothing interesting about me.

KEANE. Oh, but there is. (*Crosses to* R.) You don't know how interesting you are to me.

EMMY. But they're so much older than I am—they've had so much experience. All I know is just to be myself.

(SOPHY, *who has stood all she can, now brings a* heavy paperweight down *on the desk with a bang.* BELLE HARDWICK [U.R.] *appears in the doorway—there's a fleeting glimpse of* CHARLES *going on about his duties.* CHARLES *crosses* U.R. *to* U.L.)

BELLE. In here? . . . Hello, Sophy?

(SOPHY *rises.*)

SOPHY. Hello, Belle.

BELLE. Senator, how are you?

KEANE. How are you, Mrs. Hardwick?

EMMY. How do you do, Mrs. Hardwick?

BELLE. Hello, Emmy! Lucy not back yet, huh?

SOPHY. Not yet.

EMMY. You-all will excuse us, won't you! We're just going out riding.

BELLE. Run along.

KEANE. Good-bye, Miss Prescott. Sorry I missed Mrs. Wayne.

EMMY. Come on, Gordon. I hate to keep horses waiting. (*They go* U.R. *"Good-byes."* BELLE *stands looking after them.*)

BELLE. Good-bye!—What's that all about?

SOPHY. Love has come to the Senate. Tra-la.

BELLE. He certainly has got recuperative powers, Irene, Emmy—there's a lot of bounce to the boy.

SOPHY. Isn't there, though?

BELLE. (*Crosses to table—sits* L. *of table.*) Oh, well! Tell me: Lucy coming in soon?

SOPHY. I'm expecting her. She was at the Atwood luncheon.

BELLE. We haven't had a minute alone for ages. What's she been doing, anyhow?

SOPHY. Oh, nothing in particular.

BELLE. Don't tell *me* nothing in particular. She's up to *something*. Where *is* she all the time?

SOPHY. (*Rises.*) To tell you the truth, Belle, I don't know. She disappears for hours, and won't say a word when she comes back.

BELLE. But it's Irene, isn't?

SOPHY. What?

BELLE. (*Rises.*) It's Irene she's working on?

SOPHY. I don't know, Belle. I really don't.

BELLE. Well, I certainly hope so. Do you realize what this town would be like with Irene in the White House?

SOPHY. (*Sits at desk.*) It isn't a pleasant prospect.

BELLE. Pleasant? It's fantastic. Can you imagine her sweeping down those White House stairs at the state receptions, bowing graciously to the peasantry while the Marine Band blares out "Hail to the Chief!" I hope they don't forget some night and play "I Wonder Who's Kissing her Now." . . . Oh, well! (*A glance at the dinner plan,* U.L. *desk.*) Is that tonight's dinner?

SOPHY. Uh-huh.

BELLE. Who do *I* get?

SOPHY. Ah—let's see. You are being taken in by the great Ellsworth T. Ganning himself.

BELLE. Can't stand him.

SOPHY. Well— (*Looking over her cards*) —I can give you a Cuban attaché, unless they have a revolution before dinner.

BELLE. Oh, I'll take Ganning. (*Turn.*) I suppose as the original Hibbard man, he'll grab himself off a Cabinet place. Or will it be the Court of St. James's?

SOPHY. I think his wife prefers St. James's.

BELLE. Yes, I suppose so. That's all those New Yorkers see in politics. Those three feathers are more important to them than they are to a fan dancer. . . . Oh, hello, Lucy.

(LUCY *has entered* U.R. *She is in a state of anxious excitement, obviously keyed up even beyond her usual pitch.*)

LUCY. Hello, Belle. Sophy, did anything come for me? The mail, I mean. Did anything come for me?

SOPHY. What? (*Reaching for a little pile of letters.*) Why, no—just the usual thing.

LUCY. (*Grabbing the letters and quickly running through them*—SOPHY *hands them to* LUCY.) Oh, dear! Is this everything?

(*Enter* CHARLES U.L.)

SOPHY. Well, there were a few invitations—

LUCY. (CHARLES *takes* LUCY's *coat.*) No, no, I don't mean that.

BELLE. Listen—read your mail later and talk to *me* for a minute.

LUCY. (*To* SOPHY.) Well, did anybody call up? Long distance, I mean.

SOPHY. Why, no, I don't think so. Charles— (*He has been assisting* LUCY *with her coat*) —were there any long distance calls for Mrs. Wayne?

CHARLES. No, Miss.

(*A gesture of utter defeat from* LUCY—*she looks from one woman to the other.* CHARLES *quietly leaves the room*—U.L.)

BELLE. For heaven's sakes, Lucy, what on earth is the matter?

LUCY. (*A long breath.*) They're meeting here this afternoon.

BELLE. Who is?

LUCY. All of them. Tom, and Ganning, and Carter. They're making formal announcement in the morning. For President: Carter Hibbard.

BELLE. Well, what of it? You knew they were going to, sooner or later.

LUCY. But if I could have more time! Once he's out before the public it's ten times as hard—you know that. Even a *little* thing might stop him now if we had the right one. I'm on the track of it, but if it doesn't come today—

BELLE. What have you got?

SOPHY. What is it?

LUCY. Oh, well, it's not here, so what's the use? . . . And just to make it perfect, (*Crosses to* L.) who do you think is coming with him this afternoon? With Carter, I mean. (SOPHY *steps to* R.) The little woman to whom he owes it all, who has stood so bravely at his side through all these years.

BELLE. Not really? Irene?

LUCY. Exactly. Irene.

BELLE. When did you know this?

LUCY. Stephen called me at the luncheon.

BELLE. Did Tom know about it?

LUCY. What? I suppose so. He's coming here with Stephen.

BELLE. Then he did. He knew all about it and he didn't tell me. And I've got to pour out at Esther Blodgett's while all this is going on! "How many lumps?" (*She grimaces at an imaginary tea-drinker.*)

LUCY. You should have been at my luncheon. They were *all* lumps. (*She picks up an invitation from the table.*) ~~My God~~, the King of Egypt is having another birthday! He must be 500. (*Picking up a tray of cards on table.*) And these asinine calling cards! Obsolete anywhere else! Washington theme song: "I hear you ca-alled on me-e-e!" (*For emphasis she hurls the entire tray into the air. The cards flutter down like snow.*) Oh, I'm sorry. I'll pick them up. (BELLE *starts.*)

SOPHY. (*On her knees—picks up the cards.*) You're in a May-time mood.

BELLE. I don't blame her. It's just the way I feel.

LUCY. Then why don't you *do* something? Why do you just stand here and—

(*Enter* CHARLES U.L.)

CHARLES. Beg pardon, madam.

LUCY. (*To the* BUTLER, *who stands quietly awaiting recognition.*) Yes, Charles.

CHARLES. I just remembered, madam. Some bundles came for you this morning.

LUCY. Bundles? What sort of bundles?

CHARLES. Quite large bundles, madam. (*He indicates the size.*) They're from out of town. Cleveland.

LUCY. (*At once galvanized.*) Cleveland? That's what I am *after!* Where *are* they? Where'd you put them?

CHARLES. They're in the cellar, Madam.

LUCY. Cellar? What do you expect them to do, sprout? Get them, Charles! For heaven's sake, get them! Quick! Hurry up! (*She faces the others as a slightly bewildered* CHARLES *makes his exit.*) Cleveland! We're saved!

SOPHY. What is it?

BELLE. What have you got?

LUCY. At least I *think* we are! It's *in re* Carter Hibbard, if you know what I mean. You girls will have to excuse me if I get a little legal—there's a reason for that.

BELLE. Lucy, will you tell us what this is all about?

LUCY. Do you want to know what I've been doing all these weeks? Well, I'll tell you. I've been sitting in the Congressional Library, and I've read every decision handed down by the Supreme Court since Carter Hibbard went on it.

BELLE. Well, I don't see—

LUCY. Oh, of course you do! Because I felt pretty sure that somewhere along the line he'd stubbed his toe. I wanted a case that had to do with women—where he affronted American Womanhood. So I just sat in that mausoleum, and I read, and I read, and I read—all about easement, and chattels, and depositions—do you know that a wife can't sue her husband for a personal tort, Sophy? Well, she can't, no matter who the tort is—and I learned about competency, and estoppel, and fiduciaries, and nolle prosse and ad nauseam—there's nothing I don't know! I could pass the bar examination in any State in the Union—but I found what I was after! That's the important thing!

BELLE. What did you find?

SOPHY. Yes—what?

LUCY. The case of Mary Haggerty, God bless her. The case of Mary Haggerty versus—where's my bag? (*She reaches for the huge bag on table; dumps out its contents in one great pile. Papers and general riff-raff are scattered over the table.*) I've got it written on a card here somewhere. (*She dives into the pile.*) Belle, help me.

BELLE. (SOPHY *sits* R. *of table.*) I never saw such a mess. (*Picking up a card.*) "Sir Arthur Erskine. Minister Plenipotentiary." (*She finds another.*) "Nathan Feldstein. Send Me Your Old Rugs."

LUCY. Please, Belle!

BELLE. You've got everything here but golf sticks. . . . What's this?

LUCY. Let me see. Oh, those are Stephen's original notes on the Trans-Bulgania treaty. I want to keep those.

SOPHY. Keep them? You've never thrown anything away.

LUCY. Well, you never can tell.

BELLE. Mrs. Mary Haggerty. Is this it?

LUCY. (*Grabbing it.*) That's it! (*She reads.*) "Mrs. Mary Haggerty vs. Cleveland Interurban Railways, Inc. Ohio, 1912-'13. A.L.R., 2586." Whatever that means. (*She calls out.*) Charles, where are those bundles?

CHARLES. (*In the distance.*) Right away, Mrs. Wayne.

LUCY. Oh, if I'm only right about this! Now, here's the case. Mary Haggerty got on a Cleveland trolley car—this was way back in 1912, when Carter was on the Appellate bench out there. Anyhow, Mary got on the car, and it seems she was in what's called a delicate condition. Anyhow, too delicate for a Cleveland trolley car. Well, they came to Euclid Avenue or some place, and along came a beer truck, which was *not* in a delicate condition. (U.L.) Motorman James J. Monahan stopped the trolley car abruptly to avoid hitting the truck, and what happened? Mrs. Haggerty's baby was born in the trolley car. Prematurely, and it died. Mrs. Haggerty sued the street car company, and the Appellate Court decided against her! How's that for justice? Six to one, and you can't tell me Carter was the one! He isn't built like that.

BELLE. Well, I don't know, Lucy—

LUCY. Nonsense! Of course it was appealed to the Supreme Court—that's how I got hold of it. Only *their* records didn't name the judges—I mean out in Ohio. All it said was six to one. So I sent to Cleveland for the full report—used my pull with the Attorney General. Charles! (*But* CHARLES *is already staggering in—tugging a great roped bundle in each hand.*) Good heavens, they didn't send all that!

CHARLES. There are two more outside, Mrs. Wayne.

LUCY. Not really? But I only asked them— (SOPHY *to* C.) Sophy, where are the scissors?

SOPHY. Right here.

LUCY. You open that one.

BELLE. Lucy, this was an awfully long time ago. Do you really think—

LUCY. You bet I do! Oh, it may have been according to law, but an awful lot of women have got babies, don't forget that. Including those affiliated bodies. It's only a little bit of a thing, Belle, but it's the kind that matters to a candidate. (*She has the bundle open; extracts the top sheets.*) "Ohio Law Reports. 1906." They've sent the wrong year!

SOPHY. (*Who has opened the other bundle.*) This goes up to 1910.

LUCY. They've sent me the State archives. (*As* CHARLES *re-enters with the other two bundles—to* L. *of* LUCY U.L.)

Hurry up, Charles—it must be in one of those! (*She attacks a bundle.*) If it isn't I'll go crazy!

SOPHY. (*Still in the second bundle.*) What year did you say it was?

LUCY. What? Nineteen twelve or thirteen. Mary Haggerty versus the Cleveland Interurban Railway.

SOPHY. Here it is!

LUCY. (*Excitedly.*) Give it to me! Yes, this is it! (*Swiftly turning the pages.*) Public carrier for hire . . . not imputable to a passenger riding *in* said public carrier . . . really, they put in more talk . . . eminent domain . . . annotation . . . here we are!

BELLE. What's it say?

LUCY. Decision of the court . . . liability under constitution . . . my God, they keep *on!* . . . in consideration of— I've got it! Concurred in the result: Sloane, MacKenna, McGivney, Harris, dissenting—Justice Carter Hibbard—the dirty dog!

BELLE. Then he didn't do it?

LUCY. (*In a sunk voice.*) He voted for Mary Haggerty. He was the only one that did. The skunk!

(*There is a general relaxation.*)

BELLE. (*Sits L. of table.*) Well, that's that.

LUCY. (*Crosses to desk.*) I can't believe it. . . . Just a big humanitarian. (*Sits at desk.*) . . . Weeks in the Congressional Library . . .

(SOPHY *goes quietly to the bell* U.R. *and rings for* CHARLES. *Presently he enters* U.L.)

SOPHY. You can take these out again, Charles.

CHARLES. (*Takes last two bundles.*) Yes, miss. Shall I put them back in the cellar?

LUCY. Any place. Burn them up.

CHARLES. Yes, Mrs. Wayne. (*He carries them out.*)

LUCY. Oh, well!

(*An uncomfortable pause.*)

SOPHY. (*Scissors in hand.*) Do you want to look over the seating, Lucy?

(CHARLES *comes back for other bundles; carries them off.*)

LUCY. What?

SOPHY. Do you want to look over the seating? For tonight's dinner?

LUCY. (*Rises, crosses to back of table.*) No, I don't care *where* they sit. As far as I'm concerned, I know I'm going to get the Peruvian Ambassador. He's been here so long his country's forgotten him. A typical Washington success story —began at the bottom of the dinner table and worked up.

BELLE. (*Mumbling it over—to* LUCY.) It seems to me it would have been easier to get something on Irene, instead of Carter.

LUCY. Good Lord, haven't I tried? You don't *know* how I've tried.

BELLE. But *Irene!* There must be a dozen things.

LUCY. All right, but try to prove them! Give me *one!* There's nothing I won't use—you know that. (*She is dispiritedly putting the things back into her bag.*)

BELLE. Well, there was that South American.

LUCY. That was a week-end party. No hotel register, nothing.

BELLE. Well, Peyton Noyes. Or I'll tell you. That Spaniard —what was his name? The chargé d'affaires.

LUCY. He's back in Madrid—who knows about it? I tell you I've been over everything. Those years in Slovania or whatever it's called—when she was married to Gregoravitch —there must be something there, but what is it? Even the country's lost now—you can't *find* it since the war. It isn't on the map—I looked. . . . There's no use, Belle—she's going to be First Lady, and that's that.

BELLE. (*Rises—crosses* D.R. *Shaking her head.*) Have you seen her lately? She's practically in the White House already. Drives Carter to his office every day, walks around the golf links with him—

LUCY. Don't tell me about it. When I think what it'll do to Stephen. His whole career.

BELLE. But surely there'll always be a place for Stephen. The party can't get on without him.

LUCY. Belle, I can't let it happen. I—I just can't, that's all.

BELLE. You know, it's all wrong, really. Letting a woman be First Lady just because she happens to be married to a President.

LUCY. Of course it is. It ought to be the other way around. They ought to elect the First Lady and then let her husband be President.

BELLE. (*Sits* R. *of table.*) Do you know what she was doing today? Guest of honor at the Girl Scout House. They were cooking her a model lunch.

LUCY. Girl Scout! If I ever see that woman toasting a hot dog, I'll not be responsible.

BELLE. Well, every First Lady has to have a pet charity, and it was a toss-up between the Scouts and the Wayward Girls. She finally plunked for the Scouts.

LUCY. Too bad—she and the Wayward Girls could have had such fun swapping stories.

BELLE. Anyhow, she's getting all ready for the job. She's started to tone down the make-up—much lighter on the lipstick, and I think she'll have eyebrows again in another week.

LUCY. Oh, Belle, I don't really care about Irene any more: it's gone beyond that. But Carter, Belle—Carter Hibbard as President! We can't do that to the country. Even Keane would have been better. Oh, why did you ever tell me about Keane, anyhow? That's what started it all.

BELLE. What? What did *that* have to do with it?

LUCY. Ah—nothing. Not anything. I was just talking.

(BELLE *has been helping with the restoration of the bag; comes across the Trans-Bulgania notes.*)

BELLE. I like Stephen's handwriting, don't you? It looks like *him.*

LUCY. (*Peering over her shoulders.*) Yes, it does, doesn't it?

BELLE. (*Turning it over.*) What did you say this was? Is it important?

LUCY. (*As she takes it.*) No, not very. Trans-Bulgania. But it's important to *him.*

BELLE. (*Looking at card.*) Are you going to keep *all* this junk? Do you want the rug man?

LUCY. (*Absently, as she studies Stephen's notes.*) What?

BELLE. Do you want the rug man?

LUCY. (*Her eyes still on the notes.*) Sophy.

SOPHY. Yes?

LUCY. Where's Trans-Bulgania, exactly? Do you know?

SOPHY. (*Vaguely.*) Why, no, I don't. Over there some place.

LUCY. (*Half to herself.*) Thanks.

BELLE. (*Who has picked a batch of samples from* LUCY's *great assortment;* LUCY *goes to the telephone, picks up receiver.*) I wonder how this would look on me? (*Holding a sample to her sleeve.*)

LUCY. (*Pushes* SOPHY *aside.*) District 4510.

SOPHY. Now what? What do you want to know about *that* for?

BELLE. (*Trying another sample—a green piece.*) Or do you like this better?

LUCY. Oh, don't take that one. I want it for the couch.

BELLE. No wonder I picked it.

(SOPHY *sits down.*)

LUCY. (*Sits at desk—telephone rings.*) State Department? . . . Mr. Fleming, please. Jason Fleming.

BELLE. (*Rises—crosses a step* U.R.) Well, I suppose I'd better be on my way, or Esther Blodgett will be crazy.

LUCY. Jason? . . . This is Lucy Wayne. . . . That's right. Jason, Secretary Wayne wants to see a copy of the Trans-Bulgania Treaty. . . . That's right. Can you bring it over? . . . Oh, that'll be awfully nice of you. As soon as possible. . . . Oh, thanks. . . . (*She hangs up.*)

SOPHY. What have you got up your sleeve?

LUCY. Now, Sophy, listen. Tell Charles that when Jason Fleming comes I want him brought in *here*. In here. Is that clear?

SOPHY. No, it isn't. *Exit*

(*Enter* STEPHEN—*turn* U.E.)

LUCY. Well, never mind. Tell him anyhow.

(SOPHY *goes* D.L. *as the men enter* U.L.)

STEPHEN. Hello there, girls!

LUCY. Hello, darling. (*Kisses* STEPHEN.)

HARDWICK. What are you doing here, Belle?

BELLE. (*On her way.*) Don't Belle me. Why didn't you tell me all this was going to happen today? That Irene and Carter were coming here.

HARDWICK. Didn't know it myself till two hours ago.

BELLE. Why didn't you phone me? Irene coming here! And I've got to go to Esther Blodgett's.

LUCY. Why don't you stand out on the sidewalk, Belle, and see which one of us comes out alive?

BELLE. (*With a sigh.*) And to think I've only got Tom to describe it to me. I wish I'd married Graham McNamee. (*She goes* U.R.)

(CHARLES *enters* D.L. *with tea things.*)

STEPHEN. Well! What have you girls been up to?

LUCY. Nothing in particular. . . . Oh, Charles, did Miss Prescott give you my message?

CHARLES. (*Enter* D.L. *with tea tray.*) Yes, madam.

LUCY. Oh, I forgot to tell you, Stephen. Jason Fleming just telephoned. He wants to talk to you about the Trans-Bulgania treaty. He's bringing it over.

STEPHEN. (*Considerably puzzled.*) Trans-Bulgania. Why, that's all finished.

LUCY. (*Crosses* D.R.) (*Hastily.*) Well, something must have come up. I don't know what it is.

STEPHEN. Oh, I guess it's not important. (SOPHY *enter* D.L. *Crosses to desk, note in hand. He changes the subject, rather consciously.*) Well, ready to die for your country?

(WARN DOOR BELL.)

LUCY. (*Lightly.*) If I have to.

STEPHEN. (*Very, very serious.*) I know this isn't going to be easy for you—this afternoon, my dear. I don't like to ask it.

LUCY. Why, darling, I don't mind. How long will I have her?

STEPHEN. Well, we'll do our best. We've got to fix up an announcement—

HARDWICK. You know! "In response to an overwhelming popular demand"—

STEPHEN. Anyhow, we'll hurry it as we can. Okay?

LUCY. Okay.

STEPHEN. That's the girl. (*A little pat on the shoulder.* SOPHY *crosses* D.S., *dinner plan in hand.*) How about you, Sophy? Are you going to be around, in case—ah—

SOPHY. (*Crosses to door* D.L.) Yes, I'd planned to.

STEPHEN. That's fine.

(SOPHY *gives a knowing nod as she goes into the drawing room* D.L., *carrying the dinner plan.*)

LUCY. How you trust me! What do *you* think, Tom? Don't you think he ought to trust me more?

STEPHEN. Lucy, I don't like the way you're behaving. It makes me nervous when you're so sweet.

LUCY. Why, Stephen! That's really the most unfair remark.
                    (DOOR BELL.)

(*The door bell.*)

STEPHEN. Now—now here they are. Lucy, you've *got* to behave. This is very important. To all of us.

LUCY. (*Sweetly.*) Of course, Stephen.

HARDWICK. What's she coming here for, anyway? Why does *she* have to horn in?

STEPHEN. It wasn't my idea—it was Carter's.

LUCY. Carter's nothing! It was *hers!* Do you think *she'd* miss a chance like this?

STEPHEN. Now, you see! I know that sweetness. Lucy, you've got to do this for the party.

LUCY. (*Crosses.*) The party! I've got an idea! We'll start a *new* party! This very moment.

STEPHEN. (*Crosses to* LUCY R.) Now, Lucy!

HARDWICK. You can't start a new party now, Lucy. They're coming up the stairs.

LUCY. Oh, well, I suppose not. But something ought to be done. Oh, don't worry, Stephen—I'll behave. How can I do anything else? (*She kisses him.*)

(CHARLES *appears* U.L. *in the hallway.*)

CHARLES. Right in here, please.

(*Enter* IRENE HIBBARD, *followed immediately by* CARTER *carrying a bulky statement;* GANNING *is behind* CARTER.)

LUCY. Irene, how nice! I'm so glad to see you!

IRENE. (*With just the right note of graciousness.*) Good afternoon, Lucy.

(*The men are greeting each other.* "Hello, there, Carter!" "Stephen." "Ganning, how are you?")

LUCY. Well, Carter, this is an honor.

HIBBARD. (*With a new resonance.*) How do you do, Lucy?

LUCY. (*Approaching* GANNING.) And Warwick! the King maker! We are *indeed* honored.

GANNING. Now, Mrs. Wayne!

STEPHEN. (*Indicating a chair.*) Do sit down, Irene.

IRENE. Oh, thanks, Stephen.

LUCY. (*Waving* HIBBARD *to a chair.*) Carter.

CARTER. (*Sitting rather heavily.*) Oh, thank you.

(GANNING *too finds a chair, by desk.*)

STEPHEN. Don't get too comfortable, you fellows. We've got work to do.

LUCY. Oh, now, you can talk to us a minute. How about tea, or do you want something weaker? Carter?

HIBBARD. Ah—not now, thank you.

STEPHEN. We'll have ours upstairs.

LUCY. Oh, very well. The men will have some drinks upstairs, Charles, and you can bring tea in here.

(CHARLES *withdraws* U.L.)

IRENE. I hope you didn't mind my coming along—do you, Stephen?

STEPHEN. Why, of course not, Irene. I'm delighted.

IRENE. I felt I must be with him at this wonderful moment, this turning point in our lives. And I think he wanted me to be here. (*She turns to* CARTER.) Didn't you, dear?

HIBBARD. What? Oh, yes. Yes, my dear. (*He indulges in a little important throat clearing.*)

GANNING. I tell you, a man is only half a man when he stands alone. It takes a woman to fill him out. Don't you agree with me, Mrs. Wayne?

LUCY. Oh, yes. Yes, indeed. (*She smiles graciously at* IRENE.) Certainly you've filled Carter out.

STEPHEN. (*A bit too high, by way of saving the situation.*) Anyhow, here we all are! Seems to me we're coming out with this at just the right time—psychological moment, I should say. What do *you* think, Ganning?

GANNING. I think so. Of course, catching a newspaper reader is a very delicate operation. Very delicate.

LUCY. What do you use? Salt?

GANNING. No, no. But recently we conducted a scientific inquiry: Who is the most popular person in America?

LUCY. How interesting!

GANNING. And what was the result? The winners were Father Coughlin and Shirley Temple.

LUCY. Well, then the thing for Carter to do is to turn his collar around and wear curls.

STEPHEN. Hadn't we better go upstairs now? All ready?

GANNING. Yes, yes, of course.

HIBBARD. (*As he rises.*) At your service, gentlemen.

GANNING. (*Facing the ancestral portrait.*) You know, it seems eminently fitting that our announcement should be made from this very house, the home of Andrew Chase. Eh, Hardwick?

HARDWICK. I suppose so.

HIBBARD. (*Also lost in the portrait.*) I hope, Mrs. Wayne, that I'm able to fill his shoes.

LUCY. Oh, I'm sure you can. But of course it was the other end of Grandfather that mattered.

(CHARLES *enters with hot tea, sandwiches, cakes.*)

STEPHEN. (*Starts off* U.L.) What time do we have to give this out to catch the morning papers?

GANNING. Oh, there's no hurry. I've told our man to wait for it.

HIBBARD. (*Who finds himself with* HARDWICK *as he approaches the hallway.*) I took the liberty of preparing a little announcement for the newspapers. Sort of a tentative outline.

(*From his brief case he brings the preliminary draft—a manuscript just a little shorter than "Anthony Adverse."*)

HARDWICK. (*Taking the preliminary draft into his hand and appraising its weight.*) Hey, Stephen! Where's your bathroom scales?

(HIBBARD *exits* U.L.) (*The men are all gone.*)

LUCY. Thank you, Charles. (CHARLES *bows and goes* U.L.) Let me see. You take—ah—

IRENE. Just a little lemon, please.

LUCY. Oh, yes. (*She hands her her cup.*) Well! This is much nicer, isn't it? Just the two of us!

IRENE. Oh, much.

(*As though waiting for just this dangerous moment, which indeed she has been,* SOPHY *enters* D.L. *She pulls up a chair and sits quietly down. The watchdog.*)

LUCY. (*In mock greeting.*) How do you do, Sophy?

SOPHY. (*With a nice formality.*) How do you do?

LUCY. Will you have some tea?

SOPHY. No, thank you.

LUCY. Lemon?

SOPHY. No, thanks.

LUCY. Perhaps a spoon?

SOPHY. No, thank you.

LUCY. I see. . . . Well! (*Hands* IRENE *her tea.*) Irene? (*Sights* CHARLES *in the dining room.*) Oh, Charles! (LUCY *lights cigarette.*)

CHARLES. (*Enter* U.L.) Yes, Madame.

LUCY. Pardon me, Irene. Mr. Fleming isn't here yet, is he?

CHARLES. Not yet, Madame.

LUCY. Well, be sure to let me know.

CHARLES. Yes, Madame. (*Exits* U.L., *dining room.*)

IRENE. Ah, if you only knew how heavenly it is to have a quiet moment. I've really had the most exhausting day. Receiving this person and that. When I allow myself to think of what's ahead of me, it—it rather overwhelms me.

LUCY. Nonsense! You mustn't feel that way about it. You've had so many years of experience.

IRENE. Ah, but it's a real challenge—a challenge to any woman. Because, I don't think the White House has ever been done properly, do you?

LUCY. (*Leaning forward, rapt.*) How's that?

IRENE. Oh, I don't mean any reflection, my dear, but no one has ever preserved all its democratic traditions—because after all, this *is* a democracy—and still given it the flavor and distinction of a European court. Which it should have. Because Europe sees us through our diplomats' eyes, and judges accordingly. You see, having lived abroad for so many years, I know.

LUCY. Oh, yes, I'd forgotten about that. Whatever became of that country, anyhow? It seems to have just disappeared after you left.

IRENE. (*With a sigh.*) Oh, that horrible war! What it did to Slovania! Poor Gregoravitch lost everything—it was only a year after we were married.

LUCY. Dear me! He didn't keep it long, did he?

SOPHY. (*Doing just a little bit of rescue work.*) For my part, I think it will be very nice—having someone in the White House who really knows the ropes. I know it will make *my* life easier.

LUCY. Oh, I'm sure it will, Sophy. (*She turns to* IRENE.) You know, Sophy doesn't care who makes the laws of a nation, so long as the dinners are correctly seated.

IRENE. At least that's *one* thing you won't have to worry about for the next four years, Lucy—where you sit at the dinner table, because, of course, you're not remaining in Washington.

LUCY. I beg your pardon?

IRENE. Really, I don't know what we're going to do without you here. It'll be like Washington without the monument. Because to most people you have *become a monument*.

LUCY. Why, that's sweet of you, Irene.

IRENE. Oh, I'm sure you'll find it such a relief—living back in New York again, where no one will notice you. It'll be so restful just to be nobody.

LUCY. Well, of course you know more about that than I do.

IRENE. Ah, where you can do anything you like without having it matter. Where every time anyone says something witty it won't be attributed to you—unjustly, of course.

LUCY. Some more lemon, Irene?

IRENE. No, thank you. And Stephen, too. Freed from the pressure of public life. I do hope he'll find something to interest him.

LUCY. It's awfully good of you, Irene, to have thought so much about us.

IRENE. No, not at all.

LUCY. Because it isn't what happens to us, of course—it's what happens to *you* that counts.

IRENE. Oh, but we're all important, aren't we?

LUCY. Oh, but you'll be most important. Was that the door bell? Did I hear the door bell? (*Rises; goes toward door.*)

SOPHY. No, you didn't.

LUCY. Yes, Irene, you don't realize how important you will be.

(SOPHY *rises; stands back of chair.*)

IRENE. (*Coolly.*) I think I understand everything that the position entails.

LUCY. Oh, you can't possibly, Irene. Not until you've actually been in it—or at least seen it at close range. Of course a lot of it's wonderful—really wonderful—but you pay for it in the long run. Of course you and Carter will have to be together just the whole four years—you realize that, don't you?

IRENE. Well, I'm sure I won't mind that.

LUCY. Oh, wait. Wait till you have to campaign with him, and get up at all hours to receive bunches of wilted flowers from little girls at railway stations. Wait till you have to go to funerals with him, and lay wreaths, and unveil things. And launchings! My dear, they just never launch a battleship on a nice day—it's like open-air Shakespearean performances—you catch your death of cold every time. (SOPHY, *who sees her starting, gives an admonitory little cough. It passes quite unheeded.*)

(WARN DOOR BELL.)

Really, Irene, I must say I admire you for taking this on. There are so *many* points to consider. You take clothes alone—all those Paris frocks of yours. *They're* out, right from the beginning. (*There is a stronger and more marked cough from* SOPHY.) You've got to buy American, and you know what that means. The simplest things—that's really all you can wear. Going to the White House is like going to boarding school—all you take is your rubbers, and your raincoat, and two towels marked with your initials. (SOPHY *coughs again—still stronger.*) Why don't you take something for that, Sophy? Really, it's a grisly life. And those horrible receptions on New Year's Day—standing there forever and forever. (DOOR BELL.)
(*She waves a limp wrist by way of illustration.*) Ah! Charles! Charles! Doorbell! (CHARLES *crosses from dining*

room.) And the musicals! Hours and hours on those little gilt chairs—they leave a red line across you, right here. (*She indicates the approximate spot.*)

IRENE. (*Rising.*) Really, Lucy, you're being absurd!

LUCY. Oh, but that isn't the worst of it. It's those years after you *leave* the White House—they're what really hurt. Because there isn't any place to go after *that*. And you can't lie about your age any more, because a hundred and thirty million people know all about you. (*A step up.*) Once you've lived in the White House you're a dated egg.

IRENE. (*Her back against the wall.*) You seem to be having a very good time, Lucy. I can only suggest that you go ahead and have it *now*.

(CHARLES *appears in the hallway* U.R. *and not a second too soon.*)

CHARLES. Mr. Fleming is here, madam.

LUCY. Oh, fine. Have him come right in, Charles. He can wait in here. You don't mind, do you, Irene? Jason Fleming.

IRENE. Not in the least.

CHARLES. But he asked to see the Secretary, madam.

LUCY. Well, that's all right. He can wait in here. . . . How about some more tea? Don't you want some more tea?

IRENE. (*Crosses* L.) No, thank you.

(JASON FLEMING *appears* U.R.)

LUCY. Oh, hello, Jason. Come right in.

JASON. Mrs. Wayne. Oh, how do you do, Mrs. Hibbard? Miss Prescott.

IRENE. How do you do?

LUCY. You don't mind waiting a few minutes, do you? The Secretary's in a conference.

JASON. Not at all. (*He looks about.*) That is, if I'm not in the way.

LUCY. Why, of course not. Just the contrary. Will you have some tea? Or are you above that?

JASON. Oh, thank you very much.

IRENE. Sophy, I wonder if you could find out if the men are nearly finished.

LUCY. Oh, don't hurry off, Irene—we've only begun to talk. Lemon or cream, Jason?

JASON. Cream, please.

LUCY. (SOPHY *pushes chair back to desk.*) Why do men always take cream? I believe they think lemon is effeminate or something—*you* know, dainty little pieces like this. (*With a pair of tongs she holds a sliver of lemon aloft.*)

JASON. Well, cream isn't so virile either.

LUCY. Well, Jason, what's happening at the State Department these days? (JASON *sits on arm of chair.*) (*She addresses* IRENE.) You know, Jason gives me all the gossip— I never can get a word out of Stephen. . . . Come on, Jason. We want the inside.

JASON. Well, let's see. The Crown Princess of Egypt paid a call at the White House yesterday, and had a twenty-minute audience with the President.

LUCY. Well? That was all right, wasn't it?

JASON. Oh, fine. Except that Egypt hasn't *got* a Crown Princess.

LUCY. Oh, dear!

JASON. Of course that raised a pretty rumpus. How she got by everybody, *I* don't know. It seemed it was the State Department's fault, as usual.

LUCY. Anyhow, the Balkans are behaving these days. That's your chief worry, usually.

JASON. Yes, they're fine.

LUCY. Stephen tells me the Trans-Bulgania treaty is all ready for signing. That must be a relief to you.

JASON. Yes, that'll be a red-letter day, all right—when that's signed. We've been on it a year.

LUCY. I know—it seems forever that Stephen's been talking about it. I'd no idea it was so important.

JASON. Oh, it isn't exactly. But it makes things a lot easier for *us* boys. Business men know where they stand, for example—we don't have to answer a lot of questions every day. Such as: If I import tiddly-winks sets from Trans-Bulgania, do I have to stamp "Made in Trans-Bulgania" on every tiddly-wink?

LUCY. Well, it goes further than that, doesn't it? I was just taking a look at Stephen's notes—doesn't it have something to do with marriage laws, too?

JASON. Yes, it covers everything. It just means that from now on they recognize our laws and we recognize theirs. And boy! They've got some funny ones. Church and State are just like that over there. (*He holds up two fingers in close juxtaposition.*)

LUCY. (*Thoughtfully.*) Trans-Bulgania. Where *is* that, anyhow?

JASON. Oh, it's one of those jigsaw puzzle countries that they put together after the war. It's a union of our pre-war States, really.

LUCY. Oh, I know—sort of bits and pieces that didn't fit any place else.

JASON. That's right. Their old names were—ah—Carpathia, Vladistoya, Hohlenburg, and Slovania.

LUCY. Really? Did you say Slovania?

JASON. Oh, yes, indeed. Slovania is the largest of the four.

LUCY. Why, isn't that interesting? Irene, did you know that?

(CHARLES *appears* U.L.)

CHARLES. I beg pardon, Mr. Fleming. The Secretary wants to know if you'll come up now.

JASON. Oh, thank you, Charles. . . . (CHARLES *exits* U.L.) If you'll excuse me—

LUCY. (*Rises, crosses to* JASON.) Wait a minute, Jason. Tell me—you mean we never had a treaty with them before? Slovania.

JASON. No. Sounds funny, but we didn't.

LUCY. Well—what did we *do?* Suppose something happened to an American over there, what did we *do?*

JASON. Well, nothing, really. So far as we were concerned, it didn't happen.

LUCY. You know, this interests me awfully. I was noticing on Stephen's notes—it said something about divorce. You mean, if somebody was divorced over there, that we didn't recognize it?

JASON. That's right. Of course, it'll be different from now on.

LUCY. Then if she married someone else afterwards, would that mean—

JASON. Well, strictly speaking, she couldn't do it. It wouldn't be a marriage.

LUCY. But if she went ahead and did it anyhow, then she's been— (*She rolls the phrase pleasurably on her tongue.*)— living in sin?

JASON. That's right. So you see we *needed* a treaty. Pardon *me.* (*Exits* U.L.) (*He gives a little laugh; goes.*)

(IRENE, *of course, has been standing tense as this revelation has come forth. A caged tigress.*) (*For a moment the two women face each other, while a white-faced* SOPHY *stands in the background.*)

IRENE. You—wouldn't—dare!

LUCY. Wouldn't dare *what?*

IRENE. Wouldn't dare come out with it! With what's going on in that devilish mind of yours! It's a lie! A lie, I tell you! And I can prove it!

LUCY. Oh, no, you can't! You've been living with Carter Hibbard all these years without being married to him, and that's all there is to it. Of course, *why* you would want to *do* that, I haven't any idea.

IRENE. It's not true! Because this little squirt comes in here and says so—it's nothing but a technicality, that's all it is!

LUCY. Technicality or not, wait till the opposition paper comes out with dates, and names and places—with your marriage to Gregoravitch and a phony divorce! And photostatic copies of the phony divorce! With an interview with Gregoravitch, and another with his four wives—I'm sure the one that's in the movies will talk—and *pictures, pictures!* They'll print pictures of everything except you and Carter— and—and they may even print those! (*Her tone changes.*) After that, Irene, *nothing* will matter. You could explain till you were blue in the face, but the damage will be done. Because if a man's going to run for President of the United States, there mustn't be even a whisper *about* him! And you know it!

IRENE. It's—it's an outrage! It's unfair!

LUCY. All right, it's unfair. But it'll do the trick, just the same. How about the Church vote? Why, the party would be crazy to go ahead with him.

IRENE. (*Taking a long moment.*) I've got to think about it. I've got to have time.

LUCY. *No.* He's got to tell them today. This afternoon.

IRENE. I know why you're doing this. Don't think I don't. You want it yourself, that's why. You want it for Stephen. (*In a low tone.*) You've always been in my way, wherever I turned. You've traded on that family name of yours—you think you *own* Washington. That precious grandfather of yours! (*She looks at the portrait.*) What *was* he, anyhow? Nothing but a dirty politician! And so are you!

LUCY. (*Quite pleased.*) You bet I am. Because if I weren't you'd be in the White House.

(*The men loom up in the hallway*—STEPHEN, GANNING, HARDWICK, HIBBARD.)

STEPHEN. Well, the die is cast—meet the candidate!

IRENE. Carter! (*At the first sight of* HIBBARD, IRENE *darts quickly to him. Without a word, she pulls him into the drawing room* D.L.)

JASON. (*In the hallway* U.C.) Good-bye, Mr. Secretary!

STEPHEN. Good-bye, Jason. Sorry your trip was in vain.

JASON. Oh, that's all right. Good-bye, Mrs. Wayne.

LUCY. Oh, good-bye, Jason! And thank you very much. (*He disappears.* LUCY, *apparently for no reason at all, bursts into song—probably a bit of Italian opera.*)

STEPHEN. For God's sake, Lucy—what's the matter with you?

LUCY. Not a thing. I'm the happiest girl in the world!

GANNING. Let her alone! I feel the same way. (*He taps significantly the statement in his hand.*)

LUCY. (*On high.*) But not for the same reason.

GANNING. Where *is* Carter, anyhow?

STEPHEN. Yes, where *is* he?

GANNING. (*Peering into the next room.*) Oh, I see him. Carter!

LUCY. Yes, you'd better keep an eye on him. Because he may go out the window.

GANNING. How's that?

LUCY. Nothing, nothing!

GANNING. Carter! Carter! (CARTER HIBBARD *returns from the drawing room, followed at some distance by* IRENE. *He advances with a solemnity that at once arrests the attention of the others. His face is white.*) What's the matter? Don't you feel well?

HIBBARD. (*Painfully.*) Gentlemen—I don't quite know how to tell you this. I thought that I had been fully restored—to health—but I regret to announce that—my stomach has gone back on me. Gentlemen, I am not a candidate for the nomination.

(*There is a* "What" *from* STEPHEN, *a surprised look from* HARDWICK.)

GANNING. You're crazy! What are you talking about?

HIBBARD. I simply say that I do not feel equal to the strain of a Presidential campaign.

GANNING. But we've got everything ready. What's got into you?

HIBBARD. No, Ellsworth. No. Don't try to dissuade me. I have made up my mind. And there is no appeal from my decision. (*He goes.* IRENE *waits for a minute—surveying the room belligerently.*) Are you coming, Irene? (*Starts up.*) Irene! (*Exits* U.R.)

IRENE. (*Through her teeth.*) Yes! (*She is gone* U.R.)

(*A bewildered* GANNING *looks around at the others.*)

GANNING. I must say I don't understand that, do you?

STEPHEN. (*Slowly.*) No, I don't. What is this? Another sailors' bonus? (*His eyes go to* LUCY, *who is all innocence.*) How did the Trans-Bulgania treaty fit in?

(WARN CURTAIN.)

LUCY. (*With a smile.*) You're not old enough, dear.

HARDWICK. (*Beaming.*) Well, this sort of leaves you out on a limb, doesn't it, Ganning? A king maker, and no king.

GANNING. It's—it's monstrous. What are we going to do?

HARDWICK. You know damned well what we're going to do! There's your candidate right there! And he hasn't got a stomach either!

STEPHEN. Why, thank you, Tom. That's one of the nicest things I've ever had said about me. (*Turning to* LUCY.) Don't cry, don't cry! I haven't been elected yet.

LUCY. Kiss me anyway. (STEPHEN *kisses* LUCY.)

HARDWICK. So what do you say, Ganning? Here's your chance to get aboard the band-wagon.

GANNING. (*Taking in the situation.*) Ah—yes. Yes. You understand, Mr. Secretary, I don't want anything for myself, but *Mrs*. Ganning has always wanted to live in England. So if you see your way clear—and—

(EMMY, *flushed and excited, appears in the doorway with* KEANE.)

EMMY. (*Unable to contain herself.*) I've just got to tell you-all! Oh, excuse me, Mr. Ganning. I kind of forgot—

GANNING. Ah—how's that?

EMMY. Well—we're engaged!

LUCY. What?

EMMY. Gordon and I! We're going to be married!

LUCY. Emmy! Oh, my darling! (*Embraces her.*)

STEPHEN. Senator! My heartiest congratulations!

KEANE. Thank you, Mr. Secretary.

HARDWICK. And mine too.

GANNING. Yes, yes.

KEANE. Thank you. Thank you.

LUCY. Well, this is wonderful! To think of you and Gordon— you're going to be very, *very* happy, my dears.

KEANE. I'll do my best.

STEPHEN. Little Emmy! A Senator's wife!

EMMY. I'll just die!

HARDWICK. Senator's wife! Say, with a girl like Emmy beside him, you can't tell *where* he may go!

STEPHEN. That's right!

GANNING. Yes, there's always the White House!

HARDWICK. Sure, Emmy!

LUCY. Now don't put ideas in her head.

KEANE. (*Laughing.*) No, don't give her *that* notion! I couldn't make good on it!

EMMY. Oh, Gordon couldn't ever be President! You have to be born in the United States to be President. He wasn't born in the United States.

HARDWICK. Well, that let's *you* out, Keane.

STEPHEN. Tough luck, Emmy!

LUCY. What was that?

KEANE. Huh?

LUCY. (*In a stunned voice.*) You weren't born in the United States?

KEANE. I was born in Canada. British Columbia!

LUCY. Oh, my God.

KEANE. Why, what's the matter?

STEPHEN. You know I'm just beginning to see daylight.

(BELLE HARDWICK *rushes in from* U.R.—*a little breathless.*)

BELLE. Well, what happened? Is she gone? Tell me everything that happened.

LUCY. Not a thing, Belle—not a thing. Except that Senator Keane was born in Canada, Belle, and he can't ever be First Lady. (*Curtain starts down.*) Of course he can be Queen of England, Belle, but you never told me about that!

FAST CURTAIN

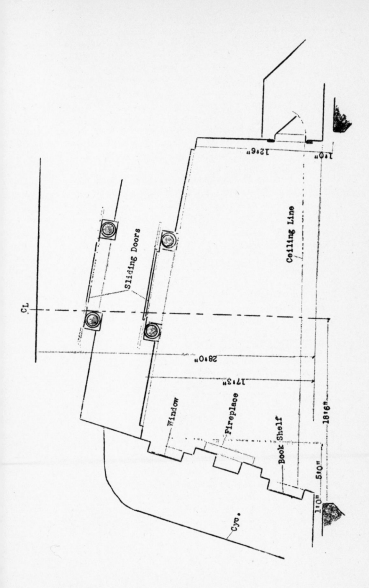

CL

Sliding Doors

Ceiling Line

Window

Fireplace

Book Shelf

Cyc.

12'6"

1'0"

28'0"

17'3"

18'6"

5'0"

1'0"

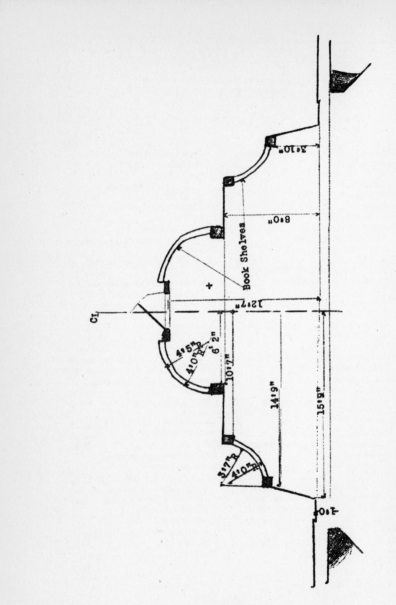

Book Shelves

3' 10"
8' 0"
12' 7"
4' 5" R
4' 0"
6' 2" R
10' 7"
14' 9"
15' 9"
3' 7" R
4' 0"
3' 0"

CL

PROPERTY PLOT

ACT I

Desk......L.C. and above door
  Desk blotter
  Hand blotter
  Ink stand
  Pencils
  Pens
  Jade ash tray
  Plain ash tray
  Book (List of senators)
  Red book
  2 small pads
  Small old-fashioned picture
  Small silver candleholder
  Telephone
  Telephone book (Washington)
  Typed Lists
  Letters (Opened—personal and
    invitations)
  Stationery
  Stationery holder
  Paper weight
  Letter opener
  Vase of flowers
  3 small vases and books to
    dress shelves
Desk chair at desk
Long table......U.L.
  2 vases of flowers — yellow
    roses
  Cigarette box
  Matches
  12 framed photos of celebrities
Landscape picture over long table
Arm chair......Below R. end of
  long table
Waste basket......at desk
Small "what-not" table..below
  pilaster L.
  Top shelf
    Vase of flowers
    China cigarette box

Ivory ash tray
Matches
Lower shelf
  3 French magazines
  2 small statues
  China cigarette box
  Bowl
Couch......U.R.
Mantelpiece-fireplace ......Right
  Clock......C.
  2 small statues L. and R. of
    clock
  2 small old-fashioned pictures
    D.S. end of mantel
  Framed photo of woman U.S.
    end
  Andirons
  Stand with poker and shovel
Bench.........front of fireplace
2 chairs......L. and R. of bench
Small table..Upstage window R.
  Vase of flowers—Lilies
  Framed photos of a general
    and The Princess of Rou-
    mania
Framed photo of The King of
  Sweden—Sill of D.S. window
Table ....................D.R.
  Candy jar-peppermints
  Cigarette box
  In cigarette box on table D.R.
    Red-tipped cigarettes in one
    compartment — plain ciga-
    rettes in other
  Card tray
    6 calling cards (see script)
  Jade ash tray
  Matches
  Letter opener
  Framed photo of Queen Marie
    of Roumania

2 arm chairs..L. and R. of table
Wing chair.......back of table
Portrait of Lucy's grandfather
   above fireplace
Large painting.......wall U.R.
2 small paintings...wall U.R.
   either side of large one
Dummy books..on shelves under
   windows R.
Drapes and curtains, windows R.
Venetian blinds....windows R.
   (¼ opened)
2 console tables, L. and R. in hall
   2 red vases—green foliage
Dining-room table........U.C.
   Large silver tray
      Coffee urn
      Creamer
      Sugar bowl
      6 cups and saucers, spoons
   Silver bowl of flowers
   Lace table cloths
   12 napkins
   Plate of sandwiches
   Plate of cakes
   Carpet
   Ground cloth for hall
OFF LEFT
3 large flower boxes (Charles)
2 corsage boxes (Sophy)

One, orchids, the other, a cor-
   sage of gardenias tied with
   blue and gold ribbon
Tea Tray (Second butler)
   Pot of tea
   Plate of sliced lemon
   Lemon fork
   Creamer
   Sugar bowl—sugar
   Sugar tongs
   6 cups, saucers, and spoons
   6 napkins
   Matches
   Small ash tray
   2 cigarettes
Small tray...........(Charles)
   Plate of crumpets
   6 plates
3 ash trays............(Sophy)
OFF RIGHT
Cup of tea, saucer, spoon, nap-
   kin, cake on top of plate
Black brief case (Stephen)
Clock strike
Door slam
PERSONAL PROPS
Lighter (Hardwick)
Matches (Keane)
Cigarette case (Irene)
Cigarettes

ACT II—SCENE I

Rug
Desk ....................D.L.
   Desk pad and blotter
   Hand blotter
   Letter opener
On desk
   Glass of water
   Small calendar
   Bottle of tablets—uncorked
   Humidor—two cigars
   Box of matches
   Washington newspaper (turned
      to comic page)
   Ink stand
   Pen

Pencils
Congressional Records
2 law briefs tied with red tape
Telephone
3 small law books
Red book (Federal Reporter)
Desk chair
Large leather chair...R. of desk
Chair ....................D.L.
Table ....................D.R.
   Detective magazine ("Murder
      in a Phone Booth")
   Geographic magazine
   Ash tray
   Matches

On shelf of table
  3 law books
2 chairs......L. and R. of table
Mounted fish on wall U.L.
Framed copy of Constitution
  ....Wall U.R.
Small framed diploma on wall
  above Constitution
Framed legal copy....Wall D.R.
Framed legal copy....Wall D.L.
Small console table..R. of alcove
  Tray—pot of coffee, cup,
  saucer, spoon, cup of Sanka,
  saucer, spoon, doily (Butler)
2 classical heads...above book-
  cases L. and R.

Classical vase....over door U.C.
Dummy books to fill bookcases
OFF LEFT
Small tray (Butler)
  Doily
  Glass of brandy
PERSONAL PROPS
Hibbard { Watch
  Chain
  Nail clipper
  Cigar clipper
  Pencil—knife—keys
Eye glasses—Hibbard
Watch—Butler

ACT II—SCENE II

Dining-room table U.C.
  4 used napkins
  Cigar
  4 used ice-cream dishes, spoons
  4 used demi-tasse cups and
  saucers
  2 ash trays
  Matches
  Bowl of red roses
  Tablecloth
  3 chairs around dining-room
  table
Chair...L. of table, turned in to
  table
  Washington evening newspaper, turned to sport page
  (over back of chair)
On desk
  Addressed letters
  Bills

Strike flowers—L. and R. in hall
Strike flowers—on table U.L.
Change flowers in vase on desk
Change flowers on table at win-
  dow U.R.
STRIKE—Card tray } table D.R.
  Calling cards }
OFF LEFT
Brief case—Sophy
Addressed letters—Sophy
OFF RIGHT
Bundle of Senate bills—Keane
Copy of statistics—Keane
PERSONAL PROPS
Small card in envelope—Emmy
Plan of dinner table—Emmy
Typed letter from Hibbard—
  Ganning (see script)
Wrist watch—Sedgwick
Wrist watch—Jason

ACT III

On Table D.R.
  Pile of Congressional Records
  Card tray
  Calling cards
  Invitation—Egyptian Embassy

Chair...L. of table turned front
On Desk L.
  Dinner plan
  8 green markers
  8 white markers

16 place cards
Box of glass slots
Pile of letters
Scissors
Small hand mirror
Red Book⎫
Letter Stand⎰ D.S. end of desk
Leather folder—in desk shelf
White flowers—in hall vases L. and R.
Change flowers—table at R. window
Change flowers—desk L.
Change flowers—"What-not" table

OFF LEFT
4 large bundles, pamphlets (2 practical)
Tray—(Charles)
2 cups, saucers, spoons
3 napkins
plate sliced lemon
lemon fork

Sugar bowl—tongs
Creamer
2 cigarettes, ash tray, matches
Tray—(Charles)
Pot of tea
Double plate (Epergne) sandwiches, cakes
Statement—(Ganning)

OFF RIGHT
Large bundle typed sheets tied red tape (Hibbard)
2 small packages (Sophy)
Vase of flowers (Charles)

PERSONAL PROPS
Cig. case⎫
Dice—playing cards⎪
Compact—powder puffs⎪ Lucy's
Packs of matches⎬ Hand
Note sheets (clipped)⎪ Bag
Calling cards⎪
Ad cards⎪
Sample material⎭